LIBRARY IN A BOOK

SUICIDE

THE FACTS ON FILE LIBRARY IN A BOOK SERIES

Each volume of the Facts On File Library in a Book series is carefully designed to be the best one-volume source for research on important current problems. Written clearly and carefully so that even the most complex aspects of the issue are easily understandable, the books give the reader the research tools to begin work, plus the information needed to delve more deeply into the topic. Each book includes a history of the subject, biographical information on important figures in the field, a complete annotated bibliography, and a carefully designed index—everything the researcher needs to get down to work.

LIBRARY IN A BOOK

SUICIDE

Stephen A. Flanders

Bibliographic materials prepared by
Mary Lou Cass, M.L.S., Rutgers University

Facts On File
New York • Oxford

LIBRARY IN A BOOK: SUICIDE

Copyright © 1991 by Stephen A. Flanders

Facts On File, Inc.   Facts On File Limited
460 Park Avenue South   Collins Street
New York NY 10016   Oxford OX4 1XJ
USA   United Kingdom

Library of Congress Cataloging-in-Publication Data
Flanders, Stephen A.
    Suicide / by Stephen A. Flanders ; bibliographic materials
prepared by Mary Lou Cass.
        p.   cm. — (Library in a book)
    Includes bibliographical references and index.
    Summary: Discusses suicide and court cases involving suicide.
Contains a bibliography and a list of pertinent associations.
    ISBN 0-8160-1909-6 (alk. paper)
    1. Suicide—Juvenile literature.   [1. Suicide.]   I. Cass, Mary
Lou.   II. Title.   III. Series.
HV6545.F54   1990
362.2'8—dc20   90-43518

A British CIP catalogue record for this book is available from the British Library.

Facts On File books are available at special discounts when purchased in bulk quantities for businesses, associations, institutions or sales promotions. Please call our Special Sales Department in New York at 212/683-2244 (dial 800/322-8755 except in NY, AK or HI) or in Oxford at 865/728399.

Text design by Ron Monteleone
Jacket design by Nadja Furlan-Lorbek
Composition by the Maple-Vail Book Composition Group
Manufactured by the Maple-Vail Book Manufacturing Group
Printed in the United States of America

10 9 8 7 6 5 4 3 2 1

This book is printed on acid-free paper.

CONTENTS

——

Contents

ACKNOWLEDGMENTS

The author would like to thank the following organizations and individuals for their assistance: the National Institute of Mental Health; the National Center for Health Statistics; the American Association of Suicidology; the American Suicide Foundation; the Youth Suicide National Center; Shirley Neitlich at the Society for the Right to Die; the Sprague Library at Montclair State College; the Montclair, New Jersey, Public Library; and Eleanora von Dehsen and Nicholas Bakalar at Facts On File.

INTRODUCTION

The purpose of this book is to provide a one-stop source for information about suicide. The first part of the book is an overview of the topic. It is designed to give the reader a basic understanding of the many aspects of self-destructive behavior. It includes a general introduction, chronology of major events, summary of important court cases, and biographical listing of key individuals.

Once acquainted with the subject of suicide, the reader can turn to the second part of the book for a comprehensive guide to reference materials on the subject. A broad spectrum of resources is identified for use in further research. At the end of the book are a listing of acronyms used throughout and a glossary of common terms.

Suicide rates in the United States are constantly changing. Knowledge about self-destructive behavior similarly continues to evolve. This book is current through December 31, 1989. Readers are encouraged to consult the reference sources in the second half of the book for developments subsequent to this date.

PART I

OVERVIEW OF THE TOPIC

CHAPTER 1

INTRODUCTION TO
SUICIDE

Approximately every 18 minutes, someone in the United States commits suicide. According to official statistics, more than 30,000 individuals take their own lives each year. Suicide ranks as the tenth leading cause of death in the United States.

Many experts believe the total number of suicides is actually much higher. Because of the social taboos that still surround the practice, it is thought many self-inflicted deaths are reported as accidents or otherwise concealed. Experts also note there are as many as ten persons who attempt to end their own lives for each one who succeeds.

In recent years there has been a marked increase in self-destructive behavior among the young. Youth suicide has become a national issue. Much of the public discussion of suicide has concerned this troubling phenomenon.

American society also has confronted the difficult question of a person's right to die. Medical advances such as mechanical respirators and artificial feeding tubes have made it possible to prolong the lives of people who otherwise would expire. At times, the ability of modern medicine to keep a person alive conflicts with that person's right to refuse intrusive life-support measures and to die with dignity. Although suicide is not countenanced by most Americans, there is growing acceptance of passive euthanasia, or the withdrawal of life-support systems, for the terminally ill. Many states have adopted living will legislation in an effort to draw a line between suicide and the right to die.

This chapter has seven sections. American attitudes about suicide are rooted in the Western cultural tradition. The first section, "Historical Background," traces both the use and study of suicide from earliest times to the present. "Suicide in the United States" then profiles the status of the practice in the nation today. "The Nature of Suicide" examines current thinking on the phenomenon of self-destructive behavior. The relationship of suicide to the law, religion, and culture is assessed in "Suicide and Society." A person's right to choose to die is addressed in "Euthanasia and the Right to Die." The status of suicide around the world is reviewed in "Worldwide Perspective." The final section, "Future Trends," discusses possible developments in the years ahead.

HISTORICAL BACKGROUND

Suicide has been a part of the human condition ever since earliest times. At one point the act of taking one's own life was thought to be linked to the development of civilization. Self-destructive behavior, however, has been reported in primitive tribes as well as in advanced industrial states. The proclivity to suicide apparently is universal, cutting across social, cultural, and ethnic lines.

Attitudes about suicide have varied widely. At different times the act has been both condemned and celebrated. In general terms, people throughout history have killed themselves for one of two reasons. In certain societies suicide was expected of their members. Such institutional suicide might take the form of the elderly sacrificing themselves for the sake of the group. Far more common, however, has been the individual suicide carried out for personal motives, ranging from love and honor to despair, disgrace, or physical pain.

For the ancient Egyptian, this motive might entail the desire to escape from the harsh realities of daily life. Death was viewed as nothing more than movement from one form of existence to another. The earliest extant writing on suicide is the Egyptian papyrus *A Dispute over Suicide* (ca. 2000 B.C.). The author, contemplating suicide, recounts his efforts to convince his soul to join him in death. Weary of life, the writer views his death as a kind of permanent vacation. His soul disagrees, observing on the one hand the various benefits to be lost along with his life, and on the other the author's social and religious responsibilities.

This debate over life and death reflected a general Egyptian neutrality toward suicide. There was no prohibition against taking one's own life— suicide was widely accepted and tolerated. In a practice later repeated by the Romans, prisoners sentenced to death were allowed to kill themselves instead.

The Old Testament likewise neither condoned nor condemned self-destructive behavior. Biblical suicides, though, were infrequent. Of the seven instances of suicide in the Old Testament, six were related to battle. Saul, the first king of Israel, fell on his sword rather than allow himself to be taken alive by his enemies. Out of loyalty, his armor-bearer followed suit. Similarly, Ahitophel, Zimri, and Razis took their own lives to avoid falling into the hands of their respective adversaries. Abimelech, whose head had been crushed by a stone reportedly thrown by a female opponent, had one of his soldiers kill him so it could not be said he was slain by a woman. The other, and best-known suicide, took place when Samson brought the Philistine temple down upon both himself and his tormentors.

Ancient Judaism in general did not approve of suicide. The act was considered an affront to God who had made the Jews his chosen people. Judaism stressed the sacredness of life and the dignity and value of each individual. There were extreme circumstances, however, when the taking of one's own life was justified. The ancient Hebrews were permitted to commit suicide to avoid betraying their faith or to escape capture and disgrace in war.

This last circumstance provoked one of the most famous mass suicides in history. In A.D. 66 a Jewish revolt broke out against Roman rule. As the rebellion crumbled, a group of Zealots, a Jewish sect noted for its religious fervor, took refuge in a fortress perched high on a desert rock formation at Masada. For two years the Zealots successfully defended their stronghold against a Roman siege. In A.D. 73, when it became apparent they could not hold out much longer, their leader, Eleazar Ben Jair, convinced the remaining 960 survivors to kill themselves rather than surrender. The Jewish faith no longer countenances such fanatical martyrdom, but Masada remains a central Jewish symbol of freedom and resistance. The Roman soldiers were said to have been deeply impressed by the discipline and indifference to death demonstrated by the Zealots.

Both the Greeks and Romans frequently committed suicide rather than face capture and humiliation in battle. Early Greek history contained several instances of mass suicides among soldiers taken prisoner who ended their own lives rather than face execution by their enemies.

Suicide for the sake of honor was widely approved in the classical world. Homer, in *The Iliad*, had Ajax kill himself rather than suffer the dishonor of not being the one to receive Achilles' armor. In one of the first Greek tragedies, *Oedipus Rex*, by Sophocles, Jocasta, Oedipus' mother, committed suicide after learning she had married her own son. The historical figure Charondas, who formulated the code of laws for the Greek colony Catania, at one point decreed that no one who was armed should

5

come to the town assembly on pain of death. When he inadvertently entered without removing his dagger, he upheld his law by drawing the weapon and using it upon himself.

The Greek myths celebrated the theme of the person driven to suicide by love or the loss of a loved one. Dido, the queen of Carthage, fell in love with Aeneas when he landed there and killed herself when he continued on his voyage. The Aegean Sea was named after Theseus' father Aegeus, who drowned himself in its waters when he mistakenly thought his son had been slain by the Minotaur. The woman Hero also drowned herself when the body of her lover, Leander, was found washed ashore. Erigone hanged herself after discovering the murdered body of her father, Icarius. Her death triggered an epidemic of similar suicidal hangings among Athenian women that lasted until a festival was instituted in her honor.

Support for sacrificing one's life for a certain nobleness of purpose, such as grief or principle, did not necessarily extend to blanket acceptance of suicide for any reason. Greek philosophy reflected the varying attitudes toward suicide. In the 6th century B.C. the Pythagoreans rejected the whole idea of suicide. They believed decisions regarding life and death were the province of the gods. Over the next several centuries a growing philosophical disenchantment with life caused a number of leading thinkers and writers to advocate suicide, maintaining it was "best to leave this world as quickly as possible."

In 403 B.C. the poison hemlock was first introduced. Athenian magistrates kept a supply on hand for those who wanted to die. All that was required was that they state their reason before the Senate, normally a formality, and obtain official permission. In the most famous suicide in antiquity, the philosopher Socrates took hemlock rather than face execution for the offense of impiety.

Plato quoted his teacher as generally opposing suicide. As he prepared to drink the hemlock, Socrates allegedly remarked that "no man has the right to take his own life, but he must wait until God sends some necessity upon him, as he has now sent me." Both Plato and his own student, Aristotle, also disapproved of suicide.

Plato likened mankind to the soldier on guard duty who must not desert his post. People were the property of the gods, who would be as angry at the self-destruction of one of their "chattel" as the average person would be at the suicide of a slave. Only in those rare instances when life itself became what Plato called "immoderate" was suicide rational and justified. Such a circumstance might involve a painful disease.

Shifting the emphasis from religion to society, Aristotle condemned suicide as an offense against the state. It weakened the moral climate and deprived society of a productive member. Self-destruction was an act of cowardice. Those who committed suicide were running away from their troubles.

Self-destruction was similarly unacceptable to the Epicureans. It did not conform to their ideal of a life dedicated to the pursuit of pleasure and the avoidance of pain. Suicide was incompatible with a philosophy that taught moderation, contemplation, and freedom from passion. If taking one's life made any sense, it was in the context that destiny was a matter of personal choice.

The Stoics took a more lenient view. Death was a release from the trials and sufferings of life. This did not mean the Stoics advocated ending one's life to escape from everyday existence. But suicide was in itself neither right nor wrong. The question was whether terminating one's life was the appropriate response in a given situation. Zeno, the founder of this philosophical school, wrote that a wise man might undertake suicide for the sake of country or friend or as a release from intolerable pain or incurable disease. Zeno was said to have killed himself at the age of 98 after interpreting a broken toe as a sign he had lived long enough. His successor, Cleanthes, was also thought to have committed suicide. He reportedly was instructed by a doctor to fast for several days, but continued to starve himself after the allotted period was over, arguing that he might as well continue on the path to death.

Stoic philosophy had a powerful influence on imperial Rome. Suicide was not generally encouraged in the early republic. By the time of the first emperors, however, acts of self-destruction took place frequently. Seneca, one of the leaders of the Roman Stoics, advocated that "If life please you, live. If not, you have a right to return whence you came." When he was charged with plotting against the emperor Nero, Seneca himself committed suicide. His wife, Paulina, not wishing to be left behind, followed suit.

Roman law reflected the fact that suicide was viewed neither with horror nor revulsion. The self-inflicted death of a private citizen was not punished, and there was no degradation of the body. It was a crime for a slave to kill himself, however, because this represented a loss for his master. Similarly, the suicide of a soldier was considered the equivalent of desertion. The soldier who survived a suicide attempt was then sentenced to death. People who were executed, unlike those who killed themselves, had their property confiscated and were denied a proper burial.

The ranks of notable suicides included Mark Antony and Cleopatra, Brutus, Cassius, Cato, Nero, and the writers Lucretius, Lucan, Terence, and Petronius. At times in the Roman Empire the act of suicide became almost routine. In a culture where thousands died in gladiatorial

---

shows, it was not uncommon for people to offer themselves for public execution in return for a sum to be paid to their heirs. The permissive attitude toward suicide of the Roman Empire did not change until Christian views began to influence and alter society.

Yet the early Christians were strongly attracted to suicide. Many welcomed their sacrifice in Roman games as a means to martyrdom and the opportunity to ascend to heaven. Any concern the potential martyrs might have for the welfare of their families was alleviated by the fact the church took care of survivors. The quest for martyrdom eventually became a kind of mania. In the 5th century St. Augustine noted that for members of the Donatist sect, "to kill themselves out of respect for martyrdom is their daily sport." Large numbers in North Africa jumped from cliffs until "the rocks below were reddened with their blood."

The new Christian faith taught that life on earth was important only as a preparation for the hereafter. The objective of daily life was to avoid sin. Those who engaged in sinful behavior risked eternal damnation. Many early Christians committed suicide out of fear of falling before temptation.

St. Augustine was the first Christian to strongly condemn suicide. In *The City of God*, he stated that the commandment "Thou shalt not kill" prohibited the taking of one's own life. No person had the right to end his life, even if it was to atone for his sins, because he was usurping the right of the church and state to punish the guilty. If an innocent man killed himself, he committed a worse sin than any he might avoid through his death because it was now impossible for him to repent. St. Augustine also adopted the Greek philosophical argument that life was the gift of God. The sufferings of life were divinely ordained and were to be borne patiently. To commit suicide was to go against the divine will.

Church leaders increasingly discouraged voluntary martyrdom, and Christian doctrine gradually moved to condemn self-destructive behavior. The Council of Orleans in 533 denied funeral rights to any person who committed suicide while accused of a crime. The seriousness of the edict rested on the belief a proper Christian burial was necessary for an individual to reach heaven. In 563 the Council of Braga forbade funeral rites for all suicides. The church further expressed its disapproval of suicide at the Council of Toledo in 693 when it ordained that those who unsuccessfully attempted to kill themselves should be excommunicated. The Synod of Nimes in 1284 extended canon law to deny to suicides the right even to interment in holy ground.

The 13th century also saw St. Thomas Aquinas articulate official church thinking on suicide in his *Summa Theologica*. Suicide was a mortal sin against God, as it was God who had given life. The act was also a sin against justice, meaning the individual's responsibilities to society, and against charity, or the individual's instinct to self-preservation. Less than 100 years later Dante, in his *Divine Comedy*, consigned the souls of those who had killed themselves to the seventh circle of hell. The souls were confined in withered trees where winged creatures, called Harpies, ceaselessly tore at them.

Throughout the medieval period the church's increasingly harsh position toward suicide dominated. Superstition and ancient folk beliefs also played a role. The practice of dishonoring the corpse of a suicide was widespread. In England the body was buried at a crossroads with a stake through the heart so that the spirit of the deceased would not return to haunt the living. The custom continued until the early 1800s, when a statute was passed abolishing the practice. In France the body of a suicide was dragged head downward through the streets and then hanged on a gallows. The body could not be taken through the door in parts of Germany but had to be passed through the window. In general, the degradation of a suicide's corpse tended to lapse by the end of the 17th century.

Beginning in the 1300s, criminal codes across Europe called for the confiscation of the goods and property of those who took their own lives. Within another 100 years, nations had begun to make suicide itself a felony. These laws of forfeiture were in effect in many places until the 1800s; suicide remained a crime in many countries well into the 20th century. In practice, though, the statutes were often circumvented. Either the death was not officially recorded as a suicide or the penalties were averted by a claim of insanity.

Despite the severe penalties, suicide did not stop in the Middle Ages. Apart from the customary individual acts of self-destruction for personal reasons, there were various instances of suicide on a larger scale. Persecution drove many Jews to kill themselves. In a terrible example, over 600 Jews took their own lives at York in England in 1190 to escape oppression. The Albigenses, a Christian sect in southern France, embraced suicide as an expression of detachment from worldly concerns. Numerous suicides occurred during the epidemics, such as the Black Plague, which swept medieval Europe.

The Renaissance brought about a transformation in attitudes toward suicide. A renewed interest in learning and the arts shifted society's emphasis from the celebration of religious themes to more secular concerns. Man and the world around him became the center of attention. The individual attained a new importance as mankind gradually realized it could control its own destiny. Society and its values began to change. Life was no longer a matter of sufferings to be borne but something to be enjoyed and appreciated.

The Reformation gave rise to the various Protestant denominations. Ideas of personal inquiry and personal responsibility replaced the absolutism and requirement for unquestioning obedience of the medieval Catholic church. The highly structured society of the Middle Ages began to come apart as beliefs and concepts that had been taken for granted were questioned and challenged.

The absolute condemnation of suicide began to fade. Erasmus, a Dutch scholar, remarked that God made death an agony "lest men far and wide commit suicide." Yet in his *Praise of Folly*, written in 1509, he defended those who would kill themselves to be free of a miserable life. In 1516, less than 200 years after the *Divine Comedy*, Sir Thomas More in his *Utopia* allowed for suicide as a kind of voluntary euthanasia. Later in the century the French essayist Montaigne revived the arguments of Seneca and other classical thinkers in favor of suicide. He finally concluded that taking one's own life was improper, but not immoral. Montaigne limited the circumstances that might justify suicide to unbearable pain or the avoidance of a worse death.

The poet, and later clergyman, John Donne wrote the first defense of suicide in English, *Biathanatos*, in 1608. Because of its controversial nature, the manuscript was not published until 1644, several years after his death. Donne argued that suicide was not incompatible with the laws of God, reason, or nature. Part of individual dignity or autonomy was the right to end one's own life. Donne also thought that the mercy of God was such that any sin connected to suicide would be forgiven.

Two of Donne's fellow clergymen likewise turned their attention to the question of self-destruction. In his *Anatomy of Melancholy*, published in 1621, Robert Burton established a relationship between melancholy and suicide. Although he condemned the act, Burton felt that eternal damnation was not necessarily the punishment for every suicide because there could be mitigating circumstances, such as madness. Burton essentially anticipated modern thinking on suicide when he identified both melancholy, or depression, and madness, or irrationality, as causes.

John Sym in his 1637 treatise, *Lifes Preservative against Self-Killing*, was the first to address the issue of suicide prevention. He divided suicide into direct and indirect forms and listed warning signs or indicators of self-destructive behavior. Sym also maintained that persons who took their own lives due to mental or emotional distress could not be held responsible for their actions.

Whether periods of great social change and flux lead to an increase in suicide is much debated. Scholars are in general agreement, however, that a rise in suicide rates occurred between the 13th and 17th centuries. It is thought that the dislocations that occurred as the feudal order came apart contributed to a sense of isolation. The loss of social cohesion, the realization by many of their dim prospects for a better future, and the growing perception of the transient nature of life itself were all factors in the melancholy described by Burton. Sym began his investigation into suicide in response to an apparent increase in self-destructive behavior in his country parish. Death in general, and suicide in particular, was a common cultural theme. Audiences for Shakespeare's plays saw suicide occur a total of 14 times in his eight tragedies.

The 18th-century Enlightenment marked a major transition in thinking about suicide. The Age of Reason emphasized empirical observation and rationality. Enlightenment thinkers were concerned with the nature of suicide and why it was that persons took their own lives. This reasoned approach challenged the traditional Christian view of suicide as a sin. The Enlightenment laid the foundation for understanding suicide as a secular rather than a religious problem. Earlier harsh treatment of suicidal behavior was rejected. Laws severely punishing the act began to change and social attitudes became more tolerant.

Considerable interest developed in the connection between the environment and suicide. The French political philosopher Montesquieu was representative of the new approach to suicide. In his *Persian Letters*, published anonymously in 1721, he defended suicide as the right of an individual to "return" the gift of life. Montesquieu characterized the laws against the practice as barbarous and unjust. He saw a cause of suicide in the climate and argued it made no sense to punish people for the effect of the environment on their behavior.

The physician George Cheyne in 1773 in *The English Malady* linked a tendency for suicide to national character. Cheyne associated the allegedly high incidence of suicide among his countrymen with the nation's dreary weather, heavy food, and increasingly urban, sedentary life-style.

The Scottish philosopher David Hume critically examined the moral arguments against suicide. In a highly influential essay, "On Suicide," published posthumously in 1783, he concluded that taking one's own life could not be considered a crime. In a frequently quoted line, Hume wrote "The life of a man is of no greater importance to the universe than that of an oyster." By this he meant suicide had no intrinsic moral value. It was not an offense against God because the Creator had given man the ability to act. God was therefore as responsible for suicide as for any other cause of death. Suicide was not a crime against society because the individual who ended his life did no actual harm but only ceased to do good. Hume also argued it was not a violation of self because no one ever committed suicide who had reason to live.

In the second half of the 18th century, two French thinkers had a significant impact on subsequent inquiry into the nature of suicide. Voltaire attacked the superstitions, taboos, and severe penalities still surrounding suicidal behavior. His analytical method and intellectual skepticism epitomized the Enlightenment's mistrust of religious thinking. In his novel *La Nouvelle Héloise*, Rousseau contended that people had a right to terminate their own lives as long as they did not harm others.

It was his thinking about the individual and society, though, that had a lasting impact on the way suicide was viewed. Rousseau believed that man in his natural state, "the noble savage," was inherently good. Mankind had acquired its wrongful behavior from society's negative influences. From here, it was not far to the idea that suicide was connected to the development of civilization or to theories linking self-destructive behavior to social experience.

The late 1700s saw dramatic changes in economic activity. The advent of the Industrial Revolution triggered rapid advances in technology that made the urbanization of the 19th century possible. The burgeoning commercialism of the time brought about a shift in attitudes toward the poor. Historically, society had not assigned a specific moral judgment to the fact of poverty. Now for the first time there was a stigma attached to being poor. Many Protestant denominations taught that prosperity was the reward of virtue. Conversely, poverty was an indication of sinfulness. The feeling of hopelessness that often accompanied being poor was thus compounded by a sense of unworthiness. The result was an upsurge in suicides, particularly among those who went from relative prosperity to poverty and suffered a corresponding loss of self-esteem.

The Romantic movement that began during this period had a powerful impact on public conceptions of death. The poet Thomas Chatterton, who lived in desperate poverty, committed suicide in 1770 at the age of 17. His death symbolized the Romantic notion of alienation from a world that no longer appreciated beauty. Goethe's *Sorrows of Young Werther*, which appeared in 1774, recounted the story of a young man driven to suicide by unrequited love. The novel sparked a "Werther" craze across Europe. Young people imitated his dress, his speech, and his self-destruction. Suicide was seen as a dramatic statement of indifference toward the dreariness of daily existence. The Romantic ideal was to suffer for the sake of art and to die young. The perceived relationship among youth, genius, and death was heightened when the poets Keats, Shelley, and Byron all died young between 1821 and 1824.

In the early 19th century there developed a general concern over rising suicide rates. The social dislocations caused by industrialization and, to a lesser extent, the Romantic fascination with poetic death were seen as the main causes. Suicide became the subject of medical and social investigation. Efforts were made to identify more precisely the conditions leading to self-destructive behavior, to develop ways to treat the suicidal patient, and to collect statistics for further research.

The introduction of statistics had a profound influence on the study of suicide. Interestingly, as the methods used to assemble and analyze these statistics became more reliable, accurate suicidal data also became more difficult to obtain. This was attributable to the growing perception of suicide as a disgrace. The middle class that emerged with the development of capitalism was frequently concerned with maintaining its social and economic status. The suicide of a family member became something that was concealed or denied. The increasing association of self-destructive behavior with insanity in the public mind only accentuated this tendency.

The medical profession searched for a connection between suicide and mental disorders. In his massive study *Mental Illness*, published in 1838, the French scientist Esquirol found that while self-destructive behavior was often a symptom of insanity, suicide itself was not a mental disease. Other factors that might influence a person to take his own life were heredity and individual disposition. Esquirol also observed that the greatest number of suicides occurred in the spring and that men killed themselves more often than women.

Another Frenchman, Falret, was the first to employ statistical data in the examination of suicide. In 1822 he released a study identifying four major causes of self-destructive behavior: predisposition, due to heredity or environment; accidental direct factors such as passion or worry; accidental indirect factors such as illness or pain; and civilization and religious fanaticism. Falret's work represented the general trend toward the recognition that suicide could result from a variety of factors.

The German physician Casper recognized the problems with suicide statistics. As early as 1825 he stressed the need to consult a variety of sources, such as police records and mortality tabulations as well as death certificates, and the importance of including attempted suicides in any analysis of the practice. Researchers such as Casper and his contemporary, Etoc-Demazy, did not focus on the individual suicide case. Their pioneering use of statistics underscored the fact that they approached suicide as a social phenomenon. Etoc-Demazy developed the use of suicide rates, rather than absolute numbers, which enabled him to establish that the tendency toward self-destructive behavior increased with age.

Bierre de Boismont undertook a massive study of 4,500 suicides over a ten-year period in his native France. He also questioned over 250 persons who had either contemplated or actually attempted taking their own lives. The leading expert on suicide in the mid-1800s, de Boismont divided the causes of self-destructive behavior into two categories: predisposing, which encompassed demographic variables such as sex or age; and determinant, which included social and behavioral factors such as poverty and alcoholism. His research confirmed higher instances of suicide among the elderly as well as among men and the unmarried.

De Boismont's conclusion that higher suicide rates were the consequence of social change and upheaval anticipated one of the most important works in the history of suicide studies: the book *Suicide* by the French sociologist Emile Durkheim. Published in 1897, this landmark study drew on the statistical methodologies developed over the preceding century. Durkheim began his analysis of self-destruction with an extensive examination of suicide statistics in France. But it was his synthesis of his conclusions into an integrated and comprehensive theory of suicide that had the greatest impact. Durkheim proposed that the causes of suicide could be defined in the relationship between the individual and society. He identified four characteristic kinds of suicide, each representing different degrees of social regulation and integration.

The four categories—altruistic, anomic, egoistic, and fatalistic—reflected his belief that social factors shaped and determined human behavior. Durkheim's ideas provoked great professional and public interest in the nature of suicide. His seminal work became the cornerstone of subsequent sociological inquiry into the subject.

Durkheim had masterfully applied the new techniques of sociology to the issue of suicide. The 20th century saw the development of another new discipline, psychoanalysis, which would dramatically alter the ways in which suicide was viewed. The psychoanalytic movement began in Vienna under the leadership of its founder, Sigmund Freud. In April 1910 members of the Vienna Psychoanalytical Society gathered to address the problem of suicide among the city's high school students. Freud left the historic meeting convinced the area of suicide required much further study.

Freud saw the internal workings of the mind as the key to human behavior. He formulated an entirely new way of looking at the human psyche. According to Freud, the mind was divided into conscious and unconscious levels. He developed a new psychoanalytic vocabulary for explaining how the various forces at play in the unconscious lay behind the ways in which people acted. Most important, it was the mind, with its unconscious elements, that was the cause of neurotic or psychotic conditions. Conflicts within the psyche were at the root of all self-destructive behavior, including suicide.

Freud first applied his psychoanalytic theories to suicide in 1917 in *Mourning and Melancholia.* He drew on his studies of these two states to arrive at a psychological explanation of self-destruction. Suicide was an instance of melancholic or depressive behavior. The potential suicide had lost interest in the outside world as well as any sense of self-esteem. Freud postulated that the self-reproach which followed the loss of self-esteem eventually culminated in a kind of desire or expectation of punishment. This punishment was fulfilled through suicide.

Freud also found that suicide involved a component of mourning. Like the mourner, the suicidal person had suffered the loss, whether perceived or real, of a loved one or object. This love object had previously been incorporated into the personality of the suicidal individual. The rage or anger against the love object brought on by its loss was also internalized. The result was an act of self-destruction.

In 1922 Freud presented a broader theory of suicide in his study *Beyond the Pleasure Principle.* Mankind had two basic instincts: Eros, or the life instinct, and Thanatos, or the death instinct. Throughout a person's life these two instincts are in constant conflict in the psyche. Although Freud developed a complicated analysis of the interplay between these instincts, suicide, in simple terms, is the triumph of Thanatos over Eros.

Freud's investigations into suicide have had a lasting impact. His classic texts remain the starting point for psychoanalytic examinations of self-destructive behavior. Freud also changed the way in which society viewed suicide. Although his theories have been much debated and criticized, the general attitude today that suicide is the result of psychological problems reaches back to Freud's monumental work in the first decades of the 20th century.

One of the first critics of Freud's ideas was his contemporary Emil Kraepelin. A German professor of psychiatry, Kraepelin believed suicide stemmed neither from social nor psychological factors. Instead, actual physical disorders underlay the depressive conditions that led to self-destructive behavior. Even though science had not yet identified the specific medical problems that caused psychiatric disorders, Kraepelin maintained it was a mistake to construct elaborate psychological theories to explain suicide. Recent discoveries in neuroscience have tended to support his observations. Studies have linked chemical imbalances in the brain to depressive behavior. More specifically, low levels of the neurotransmitter serotonin, a kind of chemical messenger in the brain, have been identified in suicidal persons.

Durkheim, Freud, and Kraepelin staked out what continue to be the broad parameters of the modern debate over the causes of suicide. Similarly, their thinking has shaped the different approaches to suicide prevention and treatment. Those who have advocated a sociological interpretation of suicide have seen cultural factors, such as cohesive and supportive communities, as essential to a reduction in self-destructive behavior.

Psychiatry has concentrated on suicide as an individual phenomenon. Psychoanalysis could identify and resolve conflicts at work in the mind of the suicidal person. Neurobiologists, on the other hand, have sought drug therapies to correct, or at least control, the chemical deficiencies in the brain to which they attribute suicidal actions.

The pioneering work of Durkheim and Freud stimulated further development of the sociological and psychological interpretations of suicide among their immediate successors. Much of this activity took place in the United States. In 1928 Ruth Cavan, a sociologist trained at the University of Chicago, published the results of a comprehensive study of self-destructive behavior in urban areas. In *Suicide*, she concluded that suicide rates were highest in neighborhoods where traditional social institutions were the most fragmented and social organizations were the weakest.

Louis Dublin, who was the chief statistician for the Metropolitan Life Insurance Company for over 40 years starting in 1911, undertook a rigorous statistical analysis of suicide in the United States. In *To Be or Not to Be*, released in 1933, he utilized sophisticated statistical models to crosstabulate age, gender, race, religion, and socioeconomic variables in deriving suicide rates and patterns. Dublin also maintained that social conditions were the basic cause of self-destructive behavior.

Both Dublin and Cavan relied on federal mortality statistics in their studies. These statistics became more precise as methods for their collection and analysis became more refined, in part through the efforts of individuals such as Dublin. However, critics of a statistical approach to suicide pointed out that the federal figures were potentially flawed. The number of reported suicides was arguably much lower than the number of actual suicides. Experts also noted there were varying degrees of severity to a suicide attempt that were difficult to quantify.

Proponents of a psychiatric approach to suicide disagreed with the emphasis on statistics for separate reasons. The psychiatrist Gregory Zilboorg dismissed the value of broad statistical analyses of suicide because they did not account for the individual psychological factors involved in each self-destructive act.

Another noted psychiatrist, Karl Menninger, also stressed that statis-

16

tics could not account for individual suicidal motives. In his 1938 book, *Man Against Himself,* he expounded on Freud's theory of the death instinct at work in each individual. Menninger stated his now-classic formulation that self-destructive behavior involved three elements: the wish to kill, the wish to be killed, and the wish to die.

Despite the growing interest in the study of suicide in the years before World War II, the act itself remained a matter to be kept out of public view. Families were reluctant to disclose that a member had taken his own life. Although it was generally accepted that suicide was related to personal problems and often was not the victim's fault, a certain measure of shame still attached to the act.

Suicide rates rose during the Great Depression of the 1930s, a fact that experts attributed to the devastating impact the economic collapse had on many lives. World War II, though, had the opposite effect. The lowest annual American suicide rate to date was recorded in 1944 when the nation was fully engaged in the armed struggle. It was assumed the intense involvement of the whole population in the outcome of the conflict, as well as the unifying experience of the war effort, tended to distract people from the personal problems that otherwise might lead them to self-destructive behavior.

Prior to World War II, the American experience with suicide had been as an individual phenomenon. The Japanese kamikaze pilots who attacked U.S. naval forces in the Pacific provided the American public with a sudden and dramatic exposure to institutional suicide. More than 1,000 young Japanese aviators died flying, or attempting to fly, their planes into Allied warships. Many Americans found it hard to comprehend that a culture would require certain of its members to deliberately sacrifice themselves for common goals. Even more difficult to understand was the willing compliance of these members.

This exposure to institutional suicide would be repeated as the United States assumed a larger role in postwar affairs and Americans came in contact with other cultures. During the Vietnam war, the evening news contained graphic footage of Buddhist monks who immolated themselves in protest against the South Vietnamese government. More recently, fundamentalist Islamic terrorists have resorted to suicide bombing attacks against Western targets in the Middle East. Intensely devout, the terrorists believe that martyrdom in this way guarantees passage to heaven.

In the years after World War II, suicide rates in the United States again began to climb. In the mid-1950s psychologists Edwin S. Shneidman and Norman L. Farberow, who were interested in suicide prevention, developed a technique, known as a "psychological autopsy," for reconstructing the sequence of factors that caused a person to kill himself. In 1958 they established the Los Angeles Suicide Prevention Center, the nation's first suicide prevention program. Shneidman and Farberow were pioneers in the emerging field of suicidology, or study of suicide. In 1968 Shneidman founded the American Association of Suicidology. The organization's primary function was the dissemination of information on suicide prevention. In addition, it promoted public awareness programs, the training of health professionals, and research into self-destructive behavior.

The new field of suicidology reflected the growing consensus that a multidisciplinary approach was necessary to understand the causes of suicide. In 1967 the sociologist Jack D. Douglas attempted in *The Social Meanings of Suicide* to link the general social conditions that were often behind self-destructive behavior with the recognition that each suicide involved unique, personal factors. Douglas argued that the impact of social events on individual behavior was ultimately determined by the meaning individuals gave those events. Statistical analyses might indicate poverty was a leading contributor to self-destructive behavior, but any theory of suicide had to take into account the fact that individuals do not all react to poverty in the same way. Subsequent suicidologists have likewise tried to synthesize the various social, psychological, and biological factors involved in suicidal behavior.

Throughout the 1960s and 1970s there was a rapidly expanding commitment of public and private resources to suicide prevention. The Los Angeles Suicide Prevention Center became the prototype for hundreds of similar facilities across the nation. Many centers established suicide hot-line numbers. Persons who were contemplating taking their own lives could call the hot line at any time for professional counsel and assistance.

The emphasis in suicide prevention was on helping individuals who were involved in unique personal crises. These individuals generally were perceived as being isolated, alone, or otherwise outside the mainstream of society. Suicide itself was not a national issue. Professionals in the health care and social service areas were concerned by the continuing high rates of suicide among the elderly. There were also indications, starting in the early 1960s, that suicide was on the rise among the young. But the broad question of suicide was not on the national agenda. Except for the self-inflicted death of a major celebrity, such as Marilyn Monroe in 1962, self-destructive behavior did not capture widespread public attention.

Two events catapulted the issue of suicide into the headlines beginning in the late 1970s. The first was the mass suicide of over 900 followers of the Reverend Jim Jones on November 18, 1978. Jones had moved his California-based People's Temple cult to the Guyana jungle in 1976.

There they had founded an agricultural settlement called Jonestown. Allegations of the mistreatment of sect members prompted an investigative visit by Congressman Leo J. Ryan. When Ryan was murdered by several cult members, Jones knew his remote settlement faced much greater scrutiny. He ordered his followers to carry out "White Night," a ritualistic mass suicide the cult had been rehearsing for months.

The horrifying event at Jonestown shocked the world. Jones was revealed as a paranoid, troubled individual who had manipulated his sect into a collective suicide pact. It was hard to grasp how more than 900 persons could willingly drink a vat of a soft drink laced with cyanide, but many ascribed the mass suicide to the bizarre behavior commonly associated with quasi-religious cult movements.

Even more difficult to understand was the sudden appearance of suicide clusters among the young. Between 1950 and 1980 the suicide rate among young persons aged 15 to 24 more than doubled. This alarming increase led in the early 1980s to a growing public concern over suicide. Numerous books, movies, and television shows began to address the problem of youth suicide. The issue gained national attention when a series of teenage suicide clusters occurred in states across the country. The term "cluster" refers to the phenomenon where one person's self-inflicted death triggers a surge of often similar suicides in the same locale. Widely reported clusters of teen suicides took place in Cheyenne; Omaha; Clear Lake City, Texas; and Westchester County, New York. In Bergenfield, New Jersey, four teenagers executed a joint suicide pact by sitting in an idling car as it filled a garage with poisonous carbon monoxide.

Experts were puzzled by the mounting number of youth suicides. Many of the young persons who took their own lives came from privileged backgrounds and seemingly had promising futures. Several private organizations, most notably the Youth Suicide National Center and the National Committee on Youth Suicide Prevention, were formed to galvanize public action in this area.

In May 1985 Secretary of Health and Human Services Margaret M. Heckler established a departmental task force on youth suicide. The federal Task Force on Youth Suicide submitted its findings in October 1987. Principal among these was the conclusion that self-destructive behavior among the young was a problem that defied ready solution. The task force recommended youth suicide be given a high priority in national health care policy.

The task force predicted that the previously articulated goal of significantly reducing the youth suicide rate by 1990 would not be attained. Since the mid-1980s, suicide rates among the young have gradually leveled off. But the incidence of youth suicide remains at record-high levels and the issue continues to be a primary concern for health care professionals, educators, and parents across the nation.

SUICIDE IN THE UNITED STATES

Who commits suicide? Every type of person. Suicide cuts across all age, racial, occupational, religious, and social groups. Almost everyone in the United States has been touched in some way by suicide. It may be through knowing an individual who committed suicide, hearing about someone in the community who did, or thinking about it personally.

Until recently, many Americans were reluctant to discuss the issue of suicide. Self-destructive behavior was considered shameful, and suicide generally was concealed or mentioned in hushed tones. This changed starting in the late 1970s with a growing recognition of a problem with youth suicide. In recent years the subject of suicide has received extensive media attention. Both the public and private sectors have taken a more active role in suicide issues. Suicide has become a matter of broad concern and interest.

This section looks at suicide in the United States today. It reviews the basic statistical data, the incidence of self-destructive behavior in different demographic groups, and the methods people choose to end their lives. The section then examines public and private involvement in the issue of suicide.

STATISTICS AND DEMOGRAPHICS

In the study of suicide, researchers rely extensively on statistics. These statistics provide a profile of self-destructive behavior in American society. They reveal whether suicide is increasing or decreasing and indicate the frequency with which the practice occurs in different groups. Before turning to a statistical portrait of suicide in the United States, it is important to understand how these statistics are derived and what their limitations are.

Suicide statistics are normally presented in two ways: numbers and rates. *Suicide numbers* identify the total volume of suicides committed by a specific group in a given period of time. The standard period of time used is a year.

An example of a suicide number would be the reported 3,295 Americans aged 20 to 24 who killed themselves in 1982. This statistic, however, does not indicate what percentage of the total number of people in this age group committed suicide. Depending on how many Americans were 20 to 24 at this time, the number 3,295 could represent either a high or low incidence of self-destructive behavior.

The percentage of those in a given group who take their own lives is expressed by a *suicide rate*. This rate is calculated in terms of 100,000 persons. So, the suicide rate of 15.1 for Americans aged 20 to 24 in 1982 means there were 15.1 suicides for every 100,000 people in this group.

Suicide statistics have become the major tool for analyzing patterns of self-destructive behavior. Over the years the methods used to accumulate and analyze the figures have been improved and refined. Still, problems exist.

The first problem is that suicides are not reported uniformly across the country. The basic record of a suicide is the death certificate. Rules vary among states on what constitutes a suicide and how it should be recorded. The determination of the coroner or medical examiner in cases where the cause of death is not clear is also a factor.

Second, the stigma attached to self-destructive behavior continues to cause families to conceal the fact of a member's suicide. The death may be reported as an accident or due to natural causes. Similarly, experts believe many seemingly accidental deaths are actually suicides. "Autocides," in which individuals camouflage their suicides in automobile accidents, are frequently cited.

Development of the psychological autopsy has helped in the identification of suicide in instances where the cause of death is uncertain. Some experts suggest, though, that the actual number of suicides may be as much as three times higher than the reported number.

Another important statistic, the number of suicide attempts, is difficult for experts to estimate. Extrapolating from various studies and reports, suicidologists calculate that unsuccessful attempts outnumber actual suicides by as much as 10 to 1. Among the young, the ratio is thought to be as high as 50 to 1. Even more challenging to approximate is the number of suicide crises, where individuals wrestle with thoughts of suicide but stop short of an actual attempt. The figures, though, are known to be high. Suicidologists believe, for example, that each year more than one million young people experience suicide crises of varying degrees.

Annual mortality statistics were first collected by the federal government in 1900. Between 1900 and 1945 suicide rates varied widely. Since then annual fluctuations in suicide rates have been much smaller. Between 1945 and 1957 the annual rate held steady at about 10.5. The year 1958 marked the beginning of a gradual upward trend in self-destructive behavior that continued until the late 1970s. Since 1978 annual rates have leveled off in the range of 12.5. Although the rates are no longer increasing, they remain at the highest levels in the postwar period.

In 1987, the most recent year for which final statistics are available, there were slightly more than 30,000 reported suicides in the United States—a rate of 12.7 for the general population. Within this overall rate, the specific rates for different groups varied considerably.

In order to identify the prevalence of suicide among the various members of a society, researchers analyze suicide rates in terms of a number of variables. The most common of these are age, sex, marital status, socioeconomic status, race, and geography. In the United States the most significant demographic factors relating to self-destructive behavior are age, sex, and race.

Elderly Suicide

The elderly historically have had the highest suicide rates. This continues to be the case, although the figures have declined slightly in recent years. In 1987 the suicide rate for people over 60 was more than 20, well above the national average. Those over 60 represent less than 20% of the population but account for roughly 30% of the suicides. Interestingly, the increasing size of the elderly population may be related to the recent flattening of suicide rates among older people. Researchers note the improved social benefits and ties that derive from greater numbers of elderly.

Youth Suicide

The suicide rate for young adults aged 15 to 24 tripled between 1958 and 1978. Since then the rate has hovered around 13, which roughly is where it stood in 1987. More than 5,000 young adults kill themselves each year. Suicide is now the third most common cause of death for adolescents aged 15 to 19 and the second leading cause for college students and those between 20 and 24.

Suicide among young children is unusual, but self-destructive behavior is not. As many as 12,000 children aged 5 to 14 are hospitalized every year for deliberate self-destructive acts, such as stabbing, burning, or taking a drug overdose.

Suicide rates traditionally have increased with age. In recent years, however, there has been a precipitous rise in the incidence of suicide among persons aged 25 to 34. The rate for individuals in this group, 15.4 in 1987, is now essentially the same as for people aged 35 to 60.

Gender

The overwhelming majority of successful suicides are committed by males. Men comprise about three-fourths of the total number of suicides each year. The suicide rate for males in 1987 was 20.5 as opposed to 5.2 for females.

Women, on the other hand, account for the preponderance of suicide attempts. An estimated three to four times more women than men attempt to kill themselves. Among young adults the ratio may be as high as 9 to 1. The reason females succeed much less often in taking their own lives is at least partly explained by the fact that they tend to choose much less lethal methods of self-destruction.

Marital Status

Married adults outnumber their single counterparts, and not surprisingly, more adult suicides occur among married people. Suicide rates, however, are higher among those who are widowed, divorced, separated, or live alone.

Socioeconomic Status

There is no established direct link between socioeconomic status and suicide. Studies indicate that self-destruction occurs equally among rich and poor. Changes in economic status, which may be a factor in suicidal behavior, can affect people from any socioeconomic group.

Race

The suicide rate for blacks and other racial minorities has averaged about half of that for whites. In 1987 the suicide rate for whites was 13.7 while the rate for all other racial groups was 6.9. The specific rate for blacks was slightly lower, at 6.6. Researchers long have noted the considerably higher suicide rates among black youths in urban areas. Many experts attribute these rates to conditions in the inner cities.

Geography

Suicide rates vary regionally in the United States. The highest rates are generally those in the Rocky Mountain and West Coast areas, while the lowest rates are found in the South. There is little difference in the incidence of suicide among urban, suburban, and rural areas.

Studies consistently have shown that age and race have little impact on the methods used in suicide. But there are considerable differences in the ways men and women seek to kill themselves.

Shooting is by far the most common means of self-inflicted death among men. Firearms are used in about 60% of male suicides. Other methods frequently employed by men include self-strangulation and poisoning.

Women historically have resorted to less lethal suicide methods, such as wrist-slashing or taking an overdose. In recent years, though, the incidence of self-inflicted gunshot wounds has increased. Among successful female suicides, firearms are now the leading cause of death. Fatal overdoses remain a close second.

Overall, more than half of all suicides are committed by firearms. In addition to strangulation and poisoning, other common methods include drowning and jumping from high places.

PUBLIC INVOLVEMENT

The principal federal agencies concerned with suicide issues are the National Institute of Mental Health (NIMH) and the Centers for Disease Control (CDC). Each is a part of the Public Health Service, which in turn comes under the Department of Health and Human Services (HHS).

A division of the Alcohol, Drug Abuse, and Mental Health Administration, the NIMH conducts research into the nature, prevention, and treatment of suicide. The agency also funds private research projects and is the primary source of federal information on self-destructive behavior.

The CDC is responsible for gathering and analyzing suicide data. The National Center for Health Statistics, a division of the CDC, collects, tabulates, and produces the national mortality statistics that include suicide numbers and rates. The CDC is involved in improving the identification and reporting of suicides. The agency also supports applied suicide research and provides technical assistance to local health departments and communities on suicide issues.

At the state and local level, public health departments perform many of the same functions. These departments normally are not involved in research efforts, but focus on prevention and treatment programs. Many local health departments operate suicide prevention centers or crisis hot lines. In many communities local school districts have initiated suicide education programs.

Suicide has not loomed as a political issue. While euthanasia and the right to die have become matters of increasing public debate, there is wide agreement that suicide itself should not be countenanced. Reflecting the growing concern in recent years over self-destructive behavior, though, Congress has conducted hearings on the problems of both elderly and youth suicide.

Historically, government agencies have been most concerned with the problem of suicide among the elderly. Various initiatives meant to provide basic human services to elderly persons, such as Social Security and Medicare, were seen as important facets of efforts to reduce elderly suicide. On a more personal level, outreach and similar programs were oriented toward socially isolated older people.

Government suicide programs have expanded their focus in response to the upsurge in youth suicide. In 1986 the NIMH cosponsored three national conferences on the issue. The conferences, which dealt with risk factors, prevention, and intervention strategies, were part of the work of the federal Task Force on Youth Suicide. Established by the Department of HHS, the task force was charged with reviewing and assessing current information on youth suicide, recommending initiatives to address the problem, and coordinating the suicide activities of federal, state, and local governments, private agencies, and professional organizations.

In its report submitted in late 1987, the task force made several recommendations. These included developing better criteria and methods for reporting suicide data, providing greater support to suicide prevention services, informing and educating the public about youth suicide, and further involving the private sector in youth suicide issues.

PRIVATE INVOLVEMENT

Over the years numerous private organizations and groups have been engaged in suicide activities. The recent emergence of the problem of youth suicide, though, has brought about a much wider private involvement in suicide issues.

The American Association of Suicidology (AAS) serves as the professional organization for individuals in the field. The association has been at the forefront of suicide research, prevention, and treatment activities. The AAS promotes education, awareness, and training programs and functions as a clearinghouse for information on suicide. Other professional organizations concerned with suicide issues as they relate to their areas of expertise include the American Medical Association, the American Psychiatric Association, and the American Psychological Association.

Concern over youth suicide led to establishment in the 1980s of the National Committee on Youth Suicide Prevention and the Youth Suicide National Center. Each of the private organizations has been active in prevention efforts. Similarly, the American Suicide Foundation was formed in 1987 to fund and otherwise support suicide research and education programs.

The media and entertainment industry have had a major impact on public awareness of suicide. The film *Ordinary People*, which won the Academy Award in 1980 for best picture, dramatically portrayed the problem of youth suicide in a seemingly normal family. In recent years each of the major television networks has aired new reports, documentaries, talk shows, and other programming on the issue of suicide in general and youth suicide in particular.

The religious community often has taken the lead in providing suicide prevention and counseling services. Both the Samaritans and CONTACT USA have a religious orientation. The organizations operate nationwide networks of prevention centers where trained volunteers are ready to befriend and assist the suicidal. Catholic Charities has sponsored self-help groups for suicide survivors in communities across the country. Other denominations and faiths have undertaken similar initiatives.

A considerable number of counseling services, self-help groups, and other outreach programs are now available to help those affected by suicide. Many of the programs stem from a combination of public and private sector initiatives. A similar mix of public and private efforts is behind the extensive number of suicide prevention centers and crisis hot lines across the nation.

THE NATURE OF SUICIDE

People take their own lives for many reasons. Some may kill themselves in response to depression or feelings of hopelessness or as a final way to escape from an intolerable situation. Others kill themselves to join a deceased loved one, to avoid the consequences of illness, or to gain attention.

Much has been learned about suicide. In recent years increasingly effective strategies have been developed for helping those who face a suicidal crisis. But as with other complex forms of human behavior, suicide is far from fully understood. Ongoing research explores areas related to its nature, prevention, and treatment.

The first part of this section, "Explanatory Theories," presents current thinking on the reasons people commit suicide. It reviews the different types of suicide and the factors associated with their occurrence. "Warning Signs" then identifies the major clues or indicators of a pending suicide. The next three parts, "Prevention," "Treatment," and "Postvention," address the various responses to self-destructive behavior. Finally, "Myths" describes the most common misconceptions about suicide.

EXPLANATORY THEORIES

Researchers have advanced numbers of theories to explain the causes of suicide. There is a large, rapidly expanding body of work on self-destructive behavior. The major theories on suicide can be categorized by the different disciplines or fields of study used in their development: sociology, psychology, and biology.

Sociology

Sociological theories of suicide emphasize the role that society and culture play in self-destructive behavior. In general, the theories focus on either social structures or social situations.

The first to propose a comprehensive sociological interpretation of suicide was the late-19th-century sociologist Emile Durkheim. He identified social structures as the key determinant in self-destructive behavior. The term "social structures" refers both to the shared values of a society and to the mechanisms in place to ensure members adhere to these values. Durkheim proposed that two basic factors in social structure, regulation and integration, heavily influence the incidence of suicide. These factors define the relationship of the individual to society, and it is this relationship that stands as suicide's underlying cause.

Durkheim postulated four characteristic forms of suicide, each the result of either too much or too little social regulation or integration. Intensely regulated societies tend to produce "fatalistic" suicides among members who feel boxed in by excessive constraints or repressive rules. On the other hand, societies that are in a state of chaos or flux are marked by "anomic" suicides among persons who cannot adjust to the changes.

"Egoistic" suicides occur among individuals who are alienated or separated from the important traditions and institutions in their society. At the other end of the integration axis is the "altruistic" suicide, where close identification of the member to the group produces a willingness to sacrifice oneself for the common good.

Durkheim greatly influenced sociological thinking on suicide. Much of the subsequent sociological work on the subject has taken a structural approach. Many have sought to connect suicide to general social factors such as an economic recession or the disintegration of communities and neighborhoods in the inner cities.

More recently, sociological theories have begun to explore the impact of social situations on self-destructive behavior. Sociologists have long maintained that social changes, such as losing a job, are a cause of suicide. The problem has been in explaining why only a small percentage

27

of those who find themselves unemployed actually take their own lives. Recent studies have tried to establish the connection between the social situations people confront and the individual decision to commit suicide. Some sociologists suggest that it is the individual's interpretation of the social situation, rather than the situation itself, that ultimately produces the suicidal act. This interpretation may be the result of complex social interactions among the people involved in the situation. Unemployment, for example, can cause considerable stress and conflict within a family.

These sociologists also acknowledge that an individual's personality may influence the interpretation of a given social situation as grounds for suicide. At this point, sociological inquiry into self-destructive behavior begins to merge with psychological interpretations of the subject.

Psychology

Psychological theories have viewed suicide as an internal matter rather than the result of external social forces. Sigmund Freud, who founded the field of psychoanalysis, also laid the groundwork for psychological thinking on self-destructive behavior.

Freud first advanced the idea that psychic forces at work in the mind are behind human behavior. He suggested that a natural impulse toward self-destruction, or death instinct, is the root cause of suicide. This instinct, located in the unconscious, is in constant conflict with the instinct for survival, or life instinct. Suicide is the result of the death instinct prevailing over the life instinct.

Freud characterized suicide as a kind of murder in reverse. Suicide was murder "in the 180th degree." When people kill themselves, they are turning inward the hostility they feel toward an outside object. Freud saw a parallel between the genesis of self-murder and the mourning process. The loss of a loved one generates ambivalent feelings, including anger and hate toward the departed. In terms of suicide, the lost loved one might be anything of importance to the individual psyche. Self-destruction is the manifestation of persons displacing these kinds of feelings back upon themselves.

Later psychological theories expanded on these ideas. The role of aggression in the suicidal act has been extensively explored. Research has looked at the phenomenon of "victim-precipitated homicide," or provoking one's own murder. Other studies have indicated that accident-proneness and excessive risk-taking reflect underlying self-destructive tendencies.

Anticipating contemporary psychological concepts, Freud connected suicide to melancholy or depression. Numerous studies have established a direct link between depression and self-destructive behavior. Recent psychological theories on suicide have emphasized the importance of personality in this equation. These theories seek to find the keys to suicide in the difference between suicidal and nonsuicidal individuals. The primary motivation at work in the suicide of persons suffering from depression is the desire to escape the condition. Certain personalities, it is argued, have a greater tendency to depression and to self-destructive behavior as the response to such depression.

There is substantial disagreement about the causes of depression. Psychoanalysis stresses the role of the individual psyche while sociology looks to events outside the person, especially social situations leading to loneliness or failure. Researchers in a third field, neurobiology, now maintain that depression is organic in origin.

Biology

Psychoanalysis is concerned with mental processes in the psyche or mind. According to traditional psychoanalytic theory, problems in human behavior derive from psychiatric disorders or neuroses. Neurobiology, in contrast, is interested in how the actual physical processes in the brain influence the ways in which people think and act. Citing recent evidence, experts in the field contend that physical disorders in the brain underlie most psychiatric problems.

Scientists now know that thoughts and feelings are generated by complex interactions of chemicals and electrical impulses between nerve cells in the brain. Communication between the nerve cells is accomplished by a group of chemical messengers called neurotransmitters. Various neurotransmitters have been linked to different behavior patterns.

In the early 1950s investigators discovered a connection between depression and abnormal levels of the neurotransmitters serotonin and norepinephrine. Antidepressant drugs were developed that increased the levels of these neurotransmitters in the brain.

Studies also connected serotonin with violent or aggressive behavior. Because of its association with both depression and aggression, it was suspected that the neurotransmitter was linked to self-destruction. In 1981 a joint team of American and Swedish researchers announced it had identified serotonin as a "suicide factor." The researchers found unusually low concentrations of the neurotransmitter in highly suicidal individuals. Subsequent studies have supported these findings.

Some neurobiologists advance a biochemical theory of suicide. Experts point out, though, that the connection among serotonin, depression, and suicide does not fully explain self-destructive behavior. No direct, causal relationship between the neurotransmitter and suicide has been established. The fact that acutely suicidal individuals have low levels of serotonin does not necessarily prove the reverse—that a deficiency in the neurotransmitter brings on self-destructive behavior. Pending further research, there is a general consensus that a low concentration of serotonin should be viewed as a possible biological marker of potential suicide.

Experts concur that there is no single explanation for suicide. In recent years the sociological, psychological, and biological investigations into self-destructive behavior have become increasingly interconnected. Current research and thinking on suicide have moved toward a multidisciplinary approach, reflecting the growing recognition that the issue involves a complex interaction of social, psychological, and biological factors.

Most experts agree on several basic factors that figure prominently in self-destructive behavior. The seven most commonly cited are:

Depression

Researchers report that 50% or more of those who kill themselves have a history of serious depression. Studies also indicate depression as a common factor among those who attempt suicide. The affective disorder most associated with suicide is "unipolar" depression. This condition is characterized by changes in behavior, dejection, and, at times, suicidal thoughts. The other affective disorder linked to self-destructive behavior, "bipolar" depression, or manic-depressive illness, is marked by impulsiveness and extreme swings in mood. The manic-depressive individual essentially cycles between periods of despair and elation. The risk of suicide is greatest when the person is experiencing an episode of despondency.

Schizophrenia

There is a high incidence of suicide attempts among people suffering from schizophrenia and other serious thought disorders. The rate is even more pronounced among people who hallucinate or are delusional. Depression also is commonly found in schizophrenic patients. Current research on the causes of schizophrenia has concentrated on chemical imbalances in the brain.

Hopelessness

Recent studies suggest that hopelessness is a central factor in suicidal behavior. Researchers investigating the attitudes of suicidal individuals have found that many are pessimistic, lack confidence in their ability to handle problems, and blame themselves for life's inevitable failures. At a certain point they feel their situation, for whatever reason, is hopeless. Suicide is perceived as the only answer.

Self-destructive behavior among persons who feel hopeless has been equated to a "cry for help." The suicide attempt is a kind of desperate, final appeal for assistance.

Alcoholism and Drug Abuse

Alcoholics have high rates of suicide and depression. It is estimated that between 7% and 21% kill themselves, compared to less than 1% of the general population. Almost 50% of the young people who commit suicide are high on alcohol or other drugs shortly before death.

Experts note that alcohol and drug abuse are often indicators of underlying depression or feelings of hopelessness. Substance abuse may serve to block out these feelings. But it can also become a kind of final trigger for a suicidal crisis. Alcohol and narcotics are mood-altering substances. Their use can cause a serious degradation of a person's thought processes and judgment. The despondent person who is thus impaired is thought to be more susceptible to self-destructive behavior.

Family Influence

Recent research has explored the strong influence families have on suicidal behavior. Studies reveal that members of a family touched by a suicide are at a greater risk for committing suicide themselves. The reasons for this are not clear. One speculation is that self-destructive behavior actually can be learned.

Abusive family situations are known to contribute to feelings of hopelessness and despair. Chaotic home environments are cited as a cause of depression and suicidal behavior in adolescents. Suicide-prone youth from difficult home situations often evidence feelings of hopelessness and worthlessness and may appear depressed and lethargic.

Illness

The psychological and emotional drains of a serious illness can lead to self-destructive behavior. The related issues of illness and independence figure prominently in suicide among the elderly. Parkinson's disease and other degenerative conditions are frequently associated with suicide. Fear over physical decline, leading to possible institutionalization, can be enough to precipitate a suicidal response among some older people.

Experts have noted high suicide rates among people with AIDS. Many individuals with the AIDS virus choose to end their own lives rather than endure the syndrome's debilitating infections.

Losses

Experts point to the loss of something important as a major reason people kill themselves. The loss may be tangible, such as a mate or friend, a job, or a person's health. It can also be something intangible. Examples include self-worth, status, or a sense of security.

Job loss can be particularly significant. Unemployment can entail the loss of important social contacts, self-esteem, and a sense of purpose as well as financial resources. For an older person, retirement can have the same impact.

In their various analyses and theories, researchers have defined the different types of suicides in a number of ways. One approach has characterized self-destruction by the motivation behind the behavior. This has produced categories such as escape suicide and revenge suicide. Suicidologists have used the terms "acute suicide" and "chronic suicide" to differentiate suicidal acts that are triggered by a specific factor and those that just seem to happen. Similarly, a distinction between direct and indirect suicide has been drawn to account for certain kinds of behavior that may lead indirectly to death, such as substance abuse.

Suicide generally is divided into two basic types. First is the *institutional* or *social suicide*. Also called conventional suicide, this form of behavior is unusual in Western societies. It involves individuals sacrificing themselves either because it is required by cultural traditions or because it is perceived as necessary for the sake of the group. The second type is the *personal* or *individual suicide*, encompassing the self-destructive acts that occur for private reasons or motivations.

In their investigations of personal suicide, suicidologists increasingly have stressed the important differences between suicide attempters and suicide completers. Many researchers view those who attempt and those who complete suicide as two distinct but overlapping groups. Attempters tend to be younger and female. Their suicidal acts are more impulsive and ambivalent. Completers generally are older males who resort to more lethal methods of self-destruction.

Experts note that the suicidal actions of many attempters are designed to gain attention. But suicidologists stress that even the most determined suicidal people normally do not want to die so much as they do not want to continue the lives they are leading. For many, whether attempters or completers, suicide is a desperate cry for help.

WARNING SIGNS

Suicidologists have established that most people who seriously contemplate suicide evidence warning signs of their intentions. Four out of five who succeed in killing themselves give clues of their pending behavior. Experts believe suicide is rarely the result of an impulsive decision. Usually the act is premeditated. The clues that a person is considering suicide can vary from a straightforward verbal hint to a subtle change in behavior.

Suicide is difficult to predict. Even experts cannot say with certainty whether or when an individual will attempt to commit suicide. Although there is no single characteristic trait in suicidal individuals, researchers have identified several warning signs that point to a greater possibility of self-destructive behavior.

Previous Suicide Attempt

This is the single best indicator of possible suicide. Individuals who have already attempted to take their own lives constitute the highest risk group for self-destructive behavior. The suicide rate for repeat attempters is more than 600 times higher than the overall rate in the general public. Follow-up studies reveal that about 10% of attempted suicides eventually go on to end their own lives. Other studies indicate that up to 65% of the people who commit suicide made prior attempts.

Suicide Talk

This is another basic indicator of suicidal intent. People who commit suicide frequently talk about it first. Statements such as "They won't have to worry about me much longer" or "They'd be better off without me" are examples of obvious threats. Experts stress that any suicide threat, including those said jokingly or in an offhand way, should be taken seriously.

Final Arrangements

Some suicidal people go about putting their affairs in order before taking their own lives. Such behavior includes making a will, giving away prized possessions, and making arrangements for pets. They often act as if they are preparing for a trip and talk about going away.

Personality or Behavior Change

A major change in personality or behavior can be a clue to possible risk for suicide. The altered personality might entail greater nervousness, angry outbursts, or apathy about appearance and health. An example of a behavior change would be a dedicated jogger who quits running. Declining school performance, such as lowered grades or missed classes, can indicate a pending youth suicide. Behavioral changes, particularly when accompanied by expressions of worthlessness or hopelessness, can be a sign of a depression severe enough to lead to self-destructive behavior.

_____

Depression

Estimates hold that one-half of the persons who take their own lives suffer from depression. The risk of a depressed individual committing suicide is roughly 50 times greater than for the general population. Clinical depression is not always easy to detect, because mood changes are part of everyday life. Symptoms of depression serious enough to contribute to suicide include:

- a change in appetite or weight
- a change in sleeping patterns
- speaking or moving with unusual speed or slowness
- a loss of interest or pleasure in usual activities
- a decrease in sexual desire
- fatigue or the loss of energy
- a diminished ability to think or concentrate
- feelings of worthlessness, self-reproach, or guilt
- a preoccupation with themes of death

Individuals who are generally alone and isolated, have few or poor social ties, abuse alcohol or drugs, or have a history of emotional difficulties are at an even higher suicide risk when clinically depressed. Often they cannot reason or think clearly. They evidence a kind of tunnel vision where every decision is cast in life-and-death terms.

The appearance of two or more warning signs together is an even clearer signal of suicidal intent. Similarly, when any of the warning signs is manifested during a period of greater stress in a person's life, there is reason for heightened concern. Events that can bring on such stress include the loss of a spouse or relative, a serious illness, a change at work, or a major move.

PREVENTION

A knowledge of the warning signs is an important facet of suicide prevention. It enables professionals and others who are concerned to recognize a potential suicide and intervene before the person actually turns to self-destructive behavior.

It is widely agreed that effective prevention, or stopping suicide before it can occur, is the key element in any response to the problem of self-destructive behavior. There is no single antidote for suicide. Over the past 40 years suicidologists and others involved in the issue have developed a range of programs and activities to minimize self-destructive behavior. The various efforts at suicide prevention fall under four headings:

research and information, education and awareness, safety precautions, and prevention centers and hot lines.

Research and Information

Why people commit suicide is the subject of extensive research. Projects funded by the NIMH are seeking to identify psychological and biological risk factors for self-destructive behavior. Once the risk factors for suicide are isolated, researchers will be able to design a profile of the potentially suicidal person. Prevention efforts then can be targeted on those who fit the high-risk profile.

Other areas of investigation also offer the promise of new prevention strategies. These include research projects on the relationship between mood disorders and suicide, the identification of possible biochemical markers for suicide, and the nature of the contagion effect in adolescent suicide.

Government agencies and private organizations are involved in disseminating information about suicide. The NIMH furnishes materials on suicide prevention and has launched a major campaign to increase public and professional knowledge about depression. State health departments likewise provide a broad spectrum of information on self-destructive behavior.

The American Association of Suicidology serves as a national clearinghouse for information on suicide. The organization's publications track the latest developments in the field of suicide prevention. Other private national organizations similarly involved in the exchange of knowledge on self-destructive behavior include the American Suicide Foundation, the Youth Suicide National Center, and the National Committee on Youth Suicide Prevention.

Education and Awareness

Experts agree that public awareness is an essential component of suicide prevention. Public awareness has several facets. At a broad level, it entails recognition of the problem of suicide and the commitment of resources to its solution. Most of the agencies and organizations involved in suicide prevention are active in public awareness campaigns. At a more personal level, awareness means that people in general are informed about self-destructive behavior and are able to help the potentially suicidal among those they know.

Numerous communities have established suicide education programs in their schools. Classes normally address the warning signs of suicide, methods of prevention, and the resources available to those in need. Many programs include courses on ways to cope with the stresses and problems of everyday life. There is also a growing trend toward including education on suicide in the professional training of physicians. Three-fourths of the people who commit suicide visit a doctor a short time before they take their own lives. More extensive instruction of physicians in self-destructive behavior could have a significant impact on suicide prevention.

Safety Precautions

Institutions where suicides are known to occur, such as psychiatric facilities and prisons, take specific precautions to prevent residents from ending their lives. Similar measures are followed in hospital areas where seriously suicidal persons are confined. Many communities identify suicide risk areas, such as high bridges, for greater surveillance. At certain popular suicide sites—the Empire State Building, for instance—physical barriers have been erected to block attempts.

Other safety precautions have been suggested. Ensuring every elderly person has a telephone has been proposed as a way of decreasing suicide among isolated older people. Some suicidologists suggest that stricter gun control laws would lower the incidence of suicides by firearms. Limiting the number of pills that can be prescribed at one time and lowering the carbon monoxide content of the gas used in homes have been cited as contributing to the recent decline in suicide rates in Great Britain.

Prevention Centers and Hot Lines

Much of the effort in suicide prevention is focused on helping those who are thinking about killing themselves. Suicide prevention centers have become the primary means for providing assistance to persons facing a suicide crisis. Since the advent of the first prevention center in Los Angeles in 1958, similar facilities have been established in communities across the nation. Most centers operate a suicide prevention hot line. Trained professionals are available to answer the calls and offer assistance as necessary.

One of the leading groups in such efforts is the Samaritans, an international nondenominational order committed to helping the suicidal. Volunteers operate 24-hour hot lines in many countries, including the United States. They also offer companionship to the lonely, distraught, and isolated. The Samaritans stress the importance of human contact and fellowship in suicide prevention. Members befriend and counsel those who come to them for assistance.

Many suicide prevention centers have expanded their activities beyond crisis intervention. Centers now train professionals and volunteers and conduct outreach programs aimed at educating the public. Most facilities are not equipped to provide long-term care. Once the immediate crisis has been handled, the acutely suicidal are referred for appropriate treatment.

TREATMENT

In recent decades the treatment of self-destructive behavior has become more effective. Health care professionals have a range of options for assisting those undergoing a suicidal crisis or who have attempted suicide. Treatment strategies include hospitalization, drug therapies, electroconvulsive therapy, and psychotherapy.

Hospitalization

For the patient who has attempted suicide, the immediate medical concern is to save the person's life. Depending on the seriousness of the attempt, this may require a range of life-saving measures. Hospitalization is normally involved.

After the immediate medical crisis is handled, the next concern is the patient's safety. Hospitalization is also used as a means of keeping a suicidal person from engaging in self-destructive behavior. Much depends on the severity of the suicidal crisis. The patient may be confined to an area where there is no access to the means to commit suicide and kept under observation.

Once the necessary safety precautions have been taken, emphasis shifts to the patient's recovery. Hospitalization can last several weeks, as it may take this long for various drug therapies and psychotherapy to begin to take effect.

Drug Therapy

In instances where the suicidal person suffers from depression, standard treatment involves the prescription of antidepressant drugs. A number of antidepressant drug therapies are available. The tricyclic antidepressants (TCA), such as imipramine and amitriptyline, are used to stablize the patient's mood and relieve depressive symptons. The monoamine oxide (MAO) inhibitors, such as isocarboxazid and phenetrine sulphate, work to control accompanying anxiety and excessive sleeping and eating. A third type of antidepressant, lithium, has proved effective in treating manic-depressive illness.

Antidepressant drugs normally are administered in combination with some form of psychotherapy. Because of their powerful impact and potentially toxic side effects, many child psychiatrists avoid using the drugs with children and, when possible, teenagers.

Electroconvulsive Therapy

In certain instances where drug therapies are not working, electroconvulsive therapy (ECT) may be used to treat severe cases of depression. Commonly referred to as electroshock therapy, this involves the application of a weak electric current to the head to induce a seizure. This is done under general anesthesia.

ECT is controversial. Although many experts in the field defend it as a safe, painless, and effective treatment for depression, its use is often avoided because it is widely perceived as an inhumane procedure. Because it can quickly dislodge a life-threatening mood, a psychiatrist may turn to ECT as an immediate treatment for a seriously suicidal person who has not responded to other therapies. ECT is not normally recommended for young people.

Improvements in ECT, such as the placement of electrodes on only one side of the head, reportedly have reduced the temporary memory loss and confusion associated with this procedure. Many psychiatrists maintain that ECT actually results in fewer complications and side effects than the use of powerful antidepressants.

Psychotherapy

There are many different types of psychotherapy. Generally, psychotherapy involves the use of specialized techniques to treat mental disorders. In terms of suicide, this means addressing the underlying mental or emotional problem that is causing the self-destructive behavior.

The psychotherapy can be short or long term. It may involve psychoanalysis or a form of counseling. Frequently family members are included in the treatment program. The suicidal person may also participate in group counseling sessions with other individuals with similar problems. Specific therapeutic strategies are available to assist patients in repairing distorted thought processes, relearning important social skills, or recapturing the confidence and desire to handle their problems.

There is no instant or automatic remedy for self-destructive behavior. Health care professionals can intervene effectively with patients in the throes of a suicide crisis. The high rate at which persons who attempt to kill themselves go on to try again, however, underscores the difficulties in suicide treatment. Experts agree that long-term follow-up care is ultimately the most important component in the treatment of self-destructive behavior.

POSTVENTION

The term "postvention" was coined by the suicidologist Dr. Edwin S. Shneidman. It refers to the assistance needed by the survivors of a suicide. This includes family members, friends, and associates of those who commit or attempt suicide as well as suicide attempters themselves.

People who survive suicide attempts require ongoing care and treatment. This normally involves counseling and other outreach programs. If the person has suffered from depression, a continuing regimen of antidepressant drugs may be prescribed. In many cases, the close relatives of the suicide attempter also receive counseling, which may include training in how to help the suicidal persons's recovery. It can also be a vehicle for assisting family members in handling their feelings of guilt, remorse, or anxiety.

A growing number of organizations have been formed to provide support to the survivors of a suicide. Thanatologists and other professionals involved in issues of death and dying observe that suicide is the most difficult bereavement crisis for a family to face and resolve. Friends and associates likewise can be deeply affected.

In most cases, the close relatives of a person who has committed suicide experience intense feelings of guilt, remorse, self-condemnation, and anger. The stress suicide causes can lead to physical exhaustion, migraines, hypertension, ulcers, and even death. The suicide of a child almost invariably has a dramatic impact on the parents. Studies have found that suicide takes its greatest toll on the children of the deceased, who undergo extended grief, confusion, and guilt. They often manifest an obsessive identification with the departed parent.

Postvention for the suicide survivor has several aspects. First is offering the bereaved emotional support and a place to express their grief. Self-help groups comprised of other suicide survivors have proved effective in aiding those who have lost a loved one. Counseling can help survivors to come to terms with the tragedy that has altered their lives. Self-help organizations and counseling facilities can also assist with the practical questions that arise. Common examples include how to explain what happened to the children, what to tell friends, or how to handle the deceased's possessions.

Family service agencies providing access to postvention programs are now found in most communities. LOSS (Loving Outreach to Survivors of a Suicide) is a nationwide network of self-help groups sponsored by Catholic Charities. Local chapters of the Compassionate Friends, a mutual support organization for the parents of children who have died, are located across the country.

MYTHS

Suicide long has been a taboo subject. Only recently has it become a matter of public discussion. Over the years a number of myths have surrounded the issue. Large numbers of people continue to believe many of these misconceptions.

Suicide experts have identified the most prevalent myths concerning self-destructive behavior in the United States today. They note that these myths, identified below, are easily refuted by modern research into the nature of suicide and will fade as public awareness of suicide continues to grow.

- "Suicidal persons are mentally ill." Suicidologists concur that persons take their own lives for a variety of reasons. Mental illness is one cause of suicide. Other factors include feelings of despondency or hopelessness and family problems.
- "Mentioning suicide may give a person the idea." Suicidal people already have the idea. Experts believe that the frank discussion of suicide may be an important component of its prevention.
- "People who talk about committing suicide don't actually attempt to do so." In fact, talk about possible self-destructive behavior is one of the warning signs of suicide.
- "A person who fails to commit suicide probably will not try again." People who have made previous suicide attempts are at the highest risk for killing themselves. A large percentage of those who succeed in taking their own lives had a history of prior attempts.
- "Nothing can stop the truly suicidal person." Advances in suicide prevention and treatment have achieved considerable success in helping persons overcome self-destructive tendencies.
- "It cannot be a suicide if there's no suicide note." Studies reveal that only about one-third of those who commit suicide leave notes.
- "They loved each other so much, they wanted to die together." Experts stress that the complex dynamics at work in suicide pacts involve much more than an expression of love.

SUICIDE AND SOCIETY

Suicide is an individual act. But as with other forms of human behavior, the meaning and significance of suicide are largely determined by society. Laws and religious beliefs define behavior as right or wrong, acceptable or unacceptable. A society's cultural expression often reveals current attitudes toward the behavior. This section examines the relationship of suicide to the law, religion, and culture. Emphasis is on the role and place of suicide in American society.

SUICIDE AND THE LAW

Following the practice in English law, the American colonies made suicide a felony in their legal codes. After independence, the individual states continued to treat both suicide and attempted suicide as crimes. The idea that the suicidal person was criminally culpable began to change as a greater understanding of self-destructive behavior evolved. Although many states had long since repealed their laws, in the late 1960s seven states still had statutes making suicide a felony. Currently no state considers either suicide or attempted suicide a crime. Aiding or abetting a suicide, however, is still widely viewed as a criminal offense.

It is against the law in most states to assist another person to commit suicide. The crime of assisted or abetted suicide normally is defined to cover either taking part in a self-destructive act or giving advice on suicide methods. Examples would include providing a loaded firearm to a suicidal person or recommending a medicine to take in a lethal overdose. It is not against the law to provide information on suicide to a general audience, such as in a book or article.

The crime of assisted suicide rarely is prosecuted. The issue of possible criminal liability is raised most often in instances where either a close relative or a medical professional helps a terminally ill person to take his own life. Unless there is evidence of financial gain or some other self-interested motive involved, the judicial system normally is reluctant to undertake criminal proceedings against a relative or loved one who may have assisted in a person's death.

Medical ethics, as well as the law, prohibit a doctor from helping a patient commit suicide. Yet in the health care field there is a general acknowledgment that it is increasingly common for physicians to directly intervene, when requested, to end the lives of their pain-wracked terminal patients.

A growing number of state courts have held that a terminally ill patient has a basic right to die. This right, however, does not extend to assisted suicide. An incurably ill patient is not entitled to request or allow another person to actively assist in bringing about death. Generally the courts have ruled that terminally ill patients do have the right to order artificial life-sustaining measures be either withheld or withdrawn. The courts have reasoned that this does not constitute suicide because the terminal illness, and not the cessation of medical procedures, is the underlying cause of death.

Two other areas that draw the law into suicide issues are life insurance and involuntary commitment. State laws generally exempt insurance companies from having to pay on a life insurance policy for someone who commits suicide within a set period of time following the issuance of the policy. The standard period is two years. After the designated time, the insurance company is required to pay regardless of the cause of death. If a policyholder dies during the "contestable period," the insurance industry normally relies on the determination on the death certificate. At times the question of whether a death was a suicide may end up in court. The law basically presumes that a person will not take his own life and the courts tend to hold for the beneficiaries.

The trend in recent years has been away from the involuntary hospitalization or confinement of a suicidal person whenever possible. There are instances, though, where health care professionals believe such action is required. Advocates of patient rights stress the importance of safeguarding the person's civil rights in such circumstances.

Most state commitment statutes require that potentially suicidal people must be both dangerous to themselves and mentally ill. This determination is made at a commitment hearing. The individual facing involuntary confinement has the right to be represented by an attorney. Normally the person's suicidal intent and mental illness are established through expert psychiatric testimony.

In 1967 California adopted the Lanterman-Petris-Short Act limiting the period of time a patient could be confined without additional proceedings. The act has become a model for similar measures in states across the nation.

SUICIDE AND RELIGION

Christian attitudes toward suicide have undergone considerable modification in the past century. Traditional Christian thinking has distinguished between the willing sacrifice of one's life and the deliberate act of killing oneself. The former is justified in instances where persons are inspired by God to perform an act of charity, mercy, or piety where death is a likely or even unavoidable consequence. Examples are ministering to the infectious sick or accepting martyrdom in defense of one's faith. Such self-sacrifice is acceptable when death itself is neither desired nor sought.

Christian teaching long has held that suicide, or the deliberate taking of one's own life, is a grave sin. It has been condemned as an offense against God, a violation of the commandment not to commit murder, and an act that precludes any chance of repentance. Official Catholic doctrine denies funeral rites or burial in consecrated ground to those who kill themselves; many Protestant denominations no longer do so.

Modern theologians have taken note of the advances in understanding the nature and causes of suicide. The major denominations continue

42

strongly to affirm that people do not have the right to take their own lives. At the same time, it is recognized that suicide is related to a range of social and psychological factors. Contemporary Christian thought increasingly has viewed self-destructive behavior as a medical issue rather than as a matter of deliberate sinfulness or evil.

Judaism also has seen suicide as a crime against God. Although sanctioned in rare instances—to avoid apostasy, for example—self-destruction generally was condemned and forbidden. The Talmud states that a suicide is not to be eulogized or publicly mourned. Each of the three denominations of modern Judaism opposes suicide. They likewise agree that it cannot be eliminated simply by religious strictures, but must be understood and actively prevented.

Islam is inalterably opposed to suicide. The Koran expressly condemns the act as the gravest sin, a crime worse than homicide. Moslems believe that an individual's destiny is preordained by God and must not be defied. Martyrdom is not viewed as suicide, but as a kind of holy mission where death is a guarantee of paradise in the next life.

Suicide generally is prohibited by Hinduism. It is permitted for individuals who have led full lives or who have attained a high level of asceticism.

Eastern religions have taken a different approach to suicide. Reflecting their emphasis on the pursuit of higher consciousness rather than the sanctity of individual life, the practice is neither opposed nor condemned. Buddhism, for example, views the human body as merely a temporary waypoint for the soul. From this perspective, suicide has no real significance.

SUICIDE AND CULTURE

Suicide has been an important cultural theme over the ages. It is found in the ancient Greek tragedies, the dramas of Shakespeare, and the works of 19th-century novelists. Customarily the portrayal of suicide in art, literature, and other cultural media has reflected the attitudes of the time.

Modern artistic expression frequently has turned to self-destruction. Films, dramas, and literary pieces have used suicide for its symbolic value or otherwise incorporated self-destructive behavior into their story lines. Twentieth-century novels as diverse as Jack London's *Martin Eden*, James Agee's *A Death in the Family*, and Carson McCuller's *The Heart Is a Lonely Hunter* have principal characters who take their own lives. Other works have directly addressed suicide as their subject. In recent years the films *Hear Me Cry*, *Silence of the Heart*, and *Surviving*, for example, have investigated the impact of suicide on its survivors.

Suicidologists have noted the high incidence of self-destruction in the artistic community. Twentieth-century American artists who took their own lives include the writers Ernest Hemingway, Hart Crane, and John Berryman; painters Jackson Pollock and Mark Rothko; and actors Marilyn Monroe and Freddie Prinze.

At times the line between life and art has become blurred. Such was the case in the Romantic period, when artistic genius was equated with early death. The Dadaist artistic movement in Paris in the 1920s began as an attack on all artistic conventions. This assault was motivated by a violent opposition to bourgeois society. The movement progressed to an attack on art in general and then on Dadaism itself. Finally the radical movement reached the point where the destruction, or suicide, of the artist was seen as necessary. Several leading Dadaists took their own lives.

In the 1950s a number of American poets began to write in what came to be known as a "confessional," or intensely personal and self-revelatory, style. Several of the poets turned to themes of their own death and dying. In her poetry and a novel, *The Bell Jar*, Sylvia Plath explored her intense preoccupation with self-destruction. She ultimately followed through on the fascination with suicide evident in her poetry when she killed herself in 1963. Her friend and fellow poet Anne Sexton later wrote that they had often talked of death. Sexton, who described her own desire to die as "the almost unnameable lust," took her own life in 1974. Their self-inflicted deaths engendered considerable debate about the relationship of the modern poet to suicide.

EUTHANASIA AND THE RIGHT TO DIE

Suicide is thought of as a tragic loss. American society dedicates substantial resources to prevent and treat self-destructive behavior. Increasingly, however, the appropriateness of suicide in some instances has become the focus of an active public debate.

The word "euthanasia" means an easy and painless death. As commonly used, it also refers to the way death is attained. Advocates of euthanasia argue that a person in intense pain or suffering should be allowed to die in a peaceful and humane way.

Euthanasia can be either voluntary or involuntary. In voluntary euthanasia, the sufferer makes the decision to hasten death and determines how this occurs. Involuntary euthanasia, or mercy killing, involves the unrequested taking of another person's life in order to spare the individual further torment.

The debate over a person's right to die centers on voluntary euthanasia. Involuntary euthanasia is widely condemned as immoral and unwarranted.

Voluntary euthanasia normally is divided into two types: active and passive. Active euthanasia involves taking direct steps to bring about death, either on one's own or with the assistance of others. Examples might include a terminally ill individual swallowing a fatal overdose or a doctor administering, when requested, a lethal injection to a dying patient.

These examples clearly are also instances of suicide. Active euthanasia does not imply that suicide in general is permissible. But it does assume the right of people in hopeless, agonizing physical conditions to end their own lives. It also presupposes the right of others to assist in the suicidal act.

Active euthanasia has been an issue throughout recorded history. At various times the practice has been both sanctioned and condemned. Passive euthanasia, by contrast, is essentially a modern phenomenon. It is directly related to advances in medical technology in this century. Artificial life-support systems have made it possible to keep alive patients who otherwise would die. In many cases there is no chance the patient will ever recover. Passive euthanasia basically amounts to allowing nature to take its course. It involves a severely ill or injured person deciding to forgo artificial life-support measures that would prolong life but would not remedy or cure the otherwise fatal condition. Passive euthanasia stops short of active measures to hasten the end of life. Instead, the terminally ill person who so desires is simply allowed to die of natural causes. There is no medical intervention to forestall death.

Whether passive euthanasia also constitutes a form of suicide has generated considerable debate. Many argue that refusing medical care is itself a form of direct action to bring about death and thus should be considered a suicidal act. The growing consensus among experts in bioethics is that when a terminally ill person declines the medical assistance necessary to stay alive, it is the underlying fatal illness and not the refusal of treatment that is the ultimate cause of death. So suicide is not involved.

Proponents of both forms of euthanasia are concerned with allowing a person to die in a dignified way. Those favoring passive euthanasia point out that in many cases artificial life-support systems accomplish little more than prolonging the agony of patients who are in the last stages of a painful, incurable disease. Many of the life-support machines, such as mechanical respirators, can inflict additional suffering. Supporters of passive euthanasia maintain that a person has a basic right to choose death over a limited and dehumanizing existence on life-support equipment.

Supporters of active euthanasia go one step further, advocating the right of individuals to receive direct help from others in ending their lives. They argue that if it is humane to let a person choose death rather than continue to exist on life-support systems, then it is just as appropriate to sanction the terminally ill to take their own lives. They reason that people who are suffering greatly should not have to endure a protracted and difficult death against their will. If help is needed to bring about death, then the medical profession should be authorized to assist as requested.

Both passive and active euthanasia are highly controversial. The issue of a person's right to die has taken on increasing significance as the use of artificial life-support systems has become more widespread. The leading advocate of passive euthanasia has been the Society for the Right to Die. Founded in 1938 as the Euthanasia Society of America, the organization has campaigned extensively in support of a right to die with dignity.

The society has been at the forefront of efforts to legalize a terminally ill person's right to refuse artificial life-support measures. In 1967 it first proposed the idea of a living will, a document in which an individual outlines in advance specific desires concerning end-of-life medical treatment. If the person later is incapacitated or otherwise unable to communicate, the living will is available to express, for example, the wish not to be kept alive by artificial means.

In 1976 California became the first state to adopt the concept of a living will when it enacted its Natural Death Act. In subsequent years numerous other states passed similar legislation authorizing the terminally ill to decline extraordinary life-support measures. By the end of 1988, 40 states had signed living will measures into law.

As the issue of passive euthanasia moved to the foreground, many in the medical profession were uncertain about the legal and ethical implications of disconnecting a patient's life-support systems. Many medical facilities were reluctant to comply with patient requests that they be allowed to die. Increasingly, the courts were called upon to resolve the difficult, and often novel, issues involved.

Also in 1976 the New Jersey Supreme Court ruled in the nation's first right-to-die case that the parents of a young woman in an irreversible coma could direct that the mechanical respirator keeping their daughter alive be withdrawn. The landmark *Quinlan* decision was the first to authorize passive euthanasia.

In subsequent right-to-die cases, courts across the country have endorsed a patient's basic right to refuse extraordinary medical care. Most of the cases have concerned people who were either terminally ill or in a persistent vegetative state with no hope of recovery. Artificial life-support systems were seen as serving only to delay the moment of death.

A limited number of right-to-die cases have addressed the right of severely handicapped people to end the medical procedures keeping them alive. Courts in several states have authorized the removal of artificial life-support equipment for paralyzed patients, reasoning that a physical condition which would result in death should life-support measures be withdrawn is the equivalent of a terminal illness. Critics of these decisions contend that the courts have actually sanctioned active euthanasia.

Western societies have traditionally prohibited active euthanasia. Such is the case in the United States today. It is a violation of medical ethnics for a doctor or other health care professional to cause the death of a patient. Assisted suicide generally is regarded as a crime. The medical professional who accedes to the request of a patient to be given a lethal injection or otherwise killed is subject to prosecution for homicide. Suicide itself is not a criminal offense, but the health care profession is bound by both legal and ethical codes to prevent a patient from taking his own life.

There is widespread opposition to active euthanasia. The American Medical Association takes the position that the involvement of a physician in the practice is a violation of the professional responsibility to do no harm. Experts in both the law and bioethics note that allowing members of the medical profession to hasten the death of a patient could easily lead to abuses. Many worry that it would place the physician in the position of playing God in life-and-death decisions.

Civic and other leaders have underscored the state's basic interest in preserving life. They stress the importance of society taking a positive stand against self-destructive behavior. Some also describe active euthanasia as a kind of Pandora's Box. They contend that once it becomes acceptable to end the lives of the terminally ill, others such as the handicapped or the very elderly may not be far behind.

The Catholic church in particular is strongly opposed to active euthanasia. Pope John Paul II has called euthanasia one of the great moral issues of the time. Official church teaching permits an individual to forgo extraordinary medical procedures when there is no hope of recovery. But assisted suicide is strongly condemned as immoral and a violation of the sanctity of life.

Unlike passive euthanasia, there is no coordinated national campaign or movement for active euthanasia. The most prominent group in support of the practice is the Hemlock Society. This national organization was formed in 1980 by Derek Humphry and his second wife, Ann Wicket. Several years earlier the two had published *Jean's Way*, an account of how Humphry helped his critically ill first wife commit suicide.

The Hemlock Society advocates the right of a person to "self-deliverance." The group believes active euthanasia should be authorized for the terminally ill and those who are severely, and incurably, physically impaired. In 1988 the organization sought unsuccessfully to obtain enough signatures to place an initiative called the Humane and Dignified Death Act as a referendum item on the ballot in California. The measure would have exempted doctors from the crime of assisted suicide in advanced, terminally ill cases.

Recent surveys indicate that support for active euthanasia is growing. Many experts suggest the practice is more widespread than generally recognized. Studies indicate that a considerable number of terminally ill patients discreetly take their own lives. It also is tacitly understood in the medical profession that many physicians accede to the pleas of terminal patients in great pain to let them die.

WORLDWIDE PERSPECTIVE

Suicide is a basic human phenomenon, occurring in every country and culture. The World Health Organization (WHO), a part of the United Nations, maintains international suicide statistics. These make possible an analysis of the incidence of suicide worldwide. It is important to note, however, that no standard international method for tracking self-destructive behavior exists. Also, many nations either are reluctant to disclose their suicide rates or lack the resources and systems necessary to record the data accurately.

The patterns of suicidal behavior in Europe and Canada basically are the same as in the United States. In general, attitudes toward suicide are more tolerant than in the past. Hungary, Austria, and Denmark are among the European nations with the highest suicide rates. West Germany as a whole has a somewhat lower rate, but West Berlin consistently has had the world's highest city suicide rate. European nations with low rates include Greece, Ireland, and Malta. Suicide statistics for Canada show little difference from those in the United States. Canada and most of the European countries have advanced suicide research, prevention, and treatment programs.

The actual suicide rate in the Soviet Union is unknown. The USSR historically has not released data to the WHO or other international health agencies. Communist ideology traditionally has described suicide as confined to bourgeois societies. Recent changes in the Soviet Union have brought about a greater openness in the discussion of social issues. Disclosures of widespread alcoholism, stemming at least in part from desperate social and economic conditions, would seem to point toward similarly elevated suicide rates.

The People's Republic of China does not disclose mortality statistics. In addition, the government apparently does not keep suicide figures. According to missionaries and other visitors, suicide was practiced widely in pre-Communist China. With the advent of a Communist government in 1948, self-destructive behavior was strictly forbidden. Many Chinese, however, took their own lives during the tumultuous Cultural Revolution in the 1960s. Recent reports from China indicate that suicide rates may be comparable to those of the industrialized nations.

The rates of suicide in Latin American countries rank among the lowest of the nations that furnish suicide rates. The traditional Catholic view of self-destructive behavior as an abomination continues to influence many of these societies, and public discussion of the subject is restrained. Authorities attribute the low suicide rates at least in part to the reluctance by many to report a death as a suicide.

Suicide is strongly condemned in the Islamic nations of the Middle East. Social prohibitions work to keep the reported suicide rates low and lead families to conceal the occurrence of self-destructive behavior. Recent suicide missions by Islamic terrorists are not a deviation from historic attitudes. Instead, they are seen within the Islamic framework as a form of martyrdom where a guarantee of transit to heaven is the reward.

Israel also has had a low incidence of suicide, although religion is not viewed as a major factor. Contemporary Judaism is far less severe than Islam in its sanctions against self-destruction.

Reliable suicide data is not available for most of Africa. Varying methods and customs involved in the reporting of deaths make any comparative study impracticable. Best estimates indicate that most African nations have low to moderate suicide rates.

In much of Asia, suicide historically was a part of everyday life. In India, Hindu beliefs directed a widow to immolate herself on her husband's funeral pyre. The ancient custom of *suttee* was outlawed by India's British rulers in 1829, but the practice endured until the early 1900s.

In Japan, the country most identified with suicide, feudal samurai warriors were bound by a strict code that often called for them to take their own lives. The Japanese ritualized suicide into an elaborate ceremony called *seppuku*, or hara-kiri. In the ceremony, the person committing suicide disemboweled himself with his own sword. Japan outlawed *seppuku* in 1868 but the tradition of honorable suicide remained an influential element in its society. In World War II Japanese kamikaze pilots flew suicide attacks against enemy warships. Many Japanese soldiers killed themselves rather than accept the humiliation of surrender.

Both exposure to Western ideas and rapid modernization have brought changes in Asian attitudes toward suicide. Since World War II, the Japanese government has supported a broad suicide prevention campaign. Suicide rates in the nation have decreased, although they remain at a level almost twice that of the United States.

FUTURE TRENDS

Human behavior is difficult to predict. Suicide is no exception. Few if any in the field foresaw the steady escalation in suicide rates for young Americans during the 1960s and 1970s. The recent decline in self-destruction among the elderly was also unanticipated.

Youth suicide rates apparently have leveled off in the past few years. Yet suicidologists are reluctant to draw broad conclusions from a relatively brief period of time. Even if youth suicide rates have stabilized, they are still at historically high levels. Indications are that elderly suicide rates may well continue to decline. Experts are much less certain about youth suicide, although there is wide agreement that any progress will be slow.

Advances in suicide prevention and treatment are most likely to come in the area of neurobiology. Research continues into the ways in which complex biochemical processes in the brain influence behavior. Scientists hope first to identify a biological marker for suicide. Recent studies have suggested that low concentrations of the neurotransmitter serotonin, already known to be connected to both depression and aggression, may have a role in suicidal behavior.

If researchers were to establish a link between a specific physical condition, such as a low level of serotonin, and self-destructive behavior, then clinicians would be able to identify and help those at risk for suicide. Drug therapies and other treatment strategies could be devised to remedy the physical condition. Experts are quick to caution, though, that even if researchers succeed in isolating a biological predisposition to suicide in some individuals, this will not by itself explain or redress the social, cultural, and psychological forces also at work in many self-destructive acts. It is expected that suicide prevention and treatment efforts will continue to involve a wide range of programs and initiatives.

Euthanasia is the issue that may well dominate the social agenda in years ahead. America's population is aging, due both to declining birth rates and increasing average lifespans. The segment of society over age 65 is expanding rapidly, both in absolute numbers and as a percentage of the overall population.

Many millions of Americans will face difficult decisions concerning their medical care. Estimates suggest that 80% of those who die today are institutionalized at the time of death. Often their lives had been prolonged by advanced medical technologies. Courts and legislatures have already been challenged by difficult and complex right-to-die issues. Experts expect continuing controversy over the circumstances in which a person may choose to die by refusing artificial life-support measures.

There also figures to be intensifying debate over the right of a terminally ill person to assisted suicide. Opinion polls indicate that a growing number of Americans favor allowing the medical profession, when requested, to hasten the death of those with agonizing incurable conditions.

CHAPTER 2

CHRONOLOGY

This chapter is a chronological account of the significant events pertaining to suicide in America since the mid-1940s. It incorporates entries drawn from a broad spectrum of medical, legal, political, social, and cultural developments. Events outside the United States that had an impact on the issue of suicide within the nation are included.

The format for entries features two cross-referencing techniques: (1) court cases in bold print are addressed in greater detail in Chapter 3; and (2) dates in parentheses, such as (Dec. 14, '85), at the end of an entry indicate related items within the chronology.

Contemporary ideas about suicide date back to the turn of the century, when two great thinkers first applied the new disciplines of sociology and psychoanalysis to the subject. As described in Chapter 1, Emile Durkheim and Sigmund Freud defined the broad parameters of subsequent inquiry into the issue of suicide. The chronology begins in 1944, when Americans for the first time confronted the seemingly incomprehensible suicide attacks of Japanese kamikaze pilots. That year also saw the lowest national suicide rate since records were first kept. Experts attributed this to the deep involvement of the average American in World War II. Since the mid-1940s, suicide rates have risen, at times dramatically. In recent years the problem of youth suicide has drawn national attention.

Developments in modern medicine in the postwar period have made it possible to prolong human life through the use of technology. Doctors, the courts, and society in general have grappled with the difficult issue of euthanasia and the right of terminally ill persons to end their own lives.

Chronology

1944

October 24: Japanese suicide pilots launch the first kamikaze attacks against U.S. naval forces during World War II.

December 31: The United States has the lowest annual suicide rate since such statistics were first collected at the turn of the century.

1945

February 13: Amid reports of widespread euthanasia in Germany, Pope Pius XII states the church's opposition to the practice in remarks to Allied medical officers.

April 15: A wave of suicides sweeps Berlin as Soviet armies advance on the city. Instances of suicide occur across Germany, particularly among Nazi officials, as the end of World War II in Europe approaches.

April 30: Adolf Hitler commits suicide in his bunker in Berlin as the Third Reich collapses. (Oct. 25, '56)

May 1: Joseph Goebbels, Nazi minister of propaganda, and his wife poison their six children and then take their own lives.

June 21: Thousands of Japanese soldiers commit suicide as American forces seize the island of Okinawa. U.S. forces encounter similar instances of suicide throughout the last year of World War II in the Far East as the strict Japanese military code stresses death over the dishonor of surrender.

June 25: The Japanese news agency reports that the civilian defense corps has received instructions to "not allow themselves to be taken prisoner alive" in the event of an invasion of the homeland.

August 3: The Lutheran Berlin Synod urges its members not to consider suicide.

October 6: The Nippon Working Masses party demands the suicide of all Japanese senior statesmen.

November 30: In Sweden 100 German military internees attempt suicide in protest against their pending deportation to the USSR. Two succeed and the remainder are hospitalized.

1946

September 27: The Euthanasia Society of America reports that 54 Protestant ministers in New York City have registered their approval of voluntary mercy deaths for the victims of painful, incurable diseases.

October 18: Mahatma Gandhi counsels Indian women to commit suicide rather than submit to dishonor.

October 19: Sentenced to death by a Nuremburg war crimes trial, Nazi leader Hermann Goering kills himself by taking poison.

1947

August 18: The National Catholic Women's Union condemns the practice of euthanasia.

December 5: A safety barrier is erected atop the Empire State Building in an attempt to prevent further suicides at the site.

December 15: A petition signed by 1,000 doctors calling for the legalization of voluntary euthanasia is sent to members of the New York State legislature.

1949

January 5: A petition signed by 379 Protestant and Jewish clergyman is sent to the New York State legislature urging enactment of a law permitting voluntary euthanasia.

January 12: The American Euthanasia Society hails Universal-International Pictures for its film *An Act of Murder*.

May 22: Former Secretary of Defense James V. Forrestal, under treatment for nervous exhaustion, leaps to his death from a window in the navy hospital in Bethesda, Maryland.

May 31: A record 121 suicides take place during the month in Tokyo, Japan. The monthly average in 1948 was 65.

1950

January 3: The United Nations is asked by 300 prominent Britons to declare euthanasia a legal right.

October 18: The World Medical Association condemns the practice of euthanasia under any circumstances.

November 28: The British government rejects a move in the House of Lords to legalize euthanasia.

1951

March 17: The British National Association for Mental Health reports that the suicide rate for Oxford undergraduates during the years 1946 to 1948 was seven times higher than for the same age group outside the university.

Chronology

1952

September 2: The World Federation for Mental Health reports higher suicide rates among immigrants than among indigenous populations.

December 9: The World Health Organization reports that Berlin has the world's highest suicide rate.

1953

February 24: Former Senator Robert M. La Follette, Jr., of Wisconsin dies of a self-inflicted bullet wound. Friends report he had been worried about his deteriorating health.

May 7: Drs. Norman L. Farberow and Edwin S. Shneidman release a six-year study of 128 war veterans that concludes that suicidal tendencies are greatest when a person seems to be recovering from emotional crisis.

November 1: The Samaritans is founded in London by the Reverend Edward Chad Varah as an unofficial Christian lay order dedicated to preventing suicide. Within 30 years the order would grow into an international organization with branches in over 40 countries.

December 28: Japan gives bonuses to families of servicemen who committed suicide upon the nation's surrender in World War II.

1954

June 19: Senator Lester C. Hunt (D, WA) fatally wounds himself at his desk in the Senate Office Building in apparent despondency over his health.

August 21: The *Asahi Evening News* reports that Tokyo's suicide rate has reached a record 54 daily.

August 24: President Getulio D. Vargas of Brazil kills himself with a pistol shot through the heart. Forced from power a few hours earlier by the military over the nation's financial crisis, Vargas left a letter to the Brazilian people in which he characterized his death as a sacrifice meant to unite them.

December 28: Over 20,000 suicides nationwide during the past year were recorded in Japan.

1956

April 13: New York medical authorities note the rising number of suicides from barbiturates.

August 11: American painter Jackson Pollock, suffering from alcoholism and depression, dies in an automobile accident in Southhampton,

New York. Authorities believed the accident was actually an instance of "autocide."

September 3: Dr. James Miller, a psychiatrist and expert on stress reactions, recommends during a symposium of the American Psychological Association that servicemen entrusted with secret information be given a suicide pill to prevent their breaking under brainwashing if captured.

September 11: In a statement to the International Congress of Catholic Doctors, Pope Pius XII bars the practice of euthanasia as contradicting the manifest law of God. (Feb. 24, '57)

October 25: Adolf Hitler's death is officially ruled a suicide by a German court. (Apr. 30, '45)

December 10: A Spokane Superior Court judge rules that the death of a marine stationed in Japan during a game of Russian roulette was a foolhardy accident rather than a suicide. As a result, his mother is authorized to collect on his life insurance.

1957

February 24: In reconfirming the church's condemnation of euthanasia, Pope Pius XII distinguishes between "ordinary" and "extraordinary" medical measures, stating that the use of extraordinary means to prolong life when there is no possibility of recovery is not necessary. (Sep. 11, '56)

July 11: The TV series *Kraft TV Theater* breaks the National Radio and TV Broadcasters Association Code with a play *The First and the Last*, showing suicide as a possible solution to a problem.

1958

February 28: Seventy-four members of the British House of Commons urge repeal of a law making suicide and attempted suicide criminal offenses. (Oct. 19, '59; Oct. 20, '60; Aug. 4, '61)

August 1: The Los Angeles Suicide Prevention Center is established by Drs. Norman L. Farberow and Edwin S. Shneidman. The Los Angeles Center becomes the prototype for suicide prevention and crisis centers throughout the world.

1959

January 22: A report to the annual conference of the American Group Psychotherapy Association scores the public apathy toward self-destructive behavior despite statistical evidence showing suicide twelve and a half times more prevalent than murder.

***February** 7:*   Rescue Inc. is formed in Boston to counsel would-be suicides.

***June** 17:*   The U.S. Health Department reports that seven persons have committed suicide with plastic bags.

***October** 19:*   The Archbishop of Canterbury states that the Church of England recommends the abolition of the British law making suicide a felony. (Feb. 28, '58; Oct. 20, '60; Aug. 4, '61)

1960

***January** 17:*   The January issue of the *Merchant Marine Council Proceedings* reports on the high incidence of suicide among U.S. merchant seamen: 34 committed suicide in 1959.

***January** 22:*   Senator A. S. Mike Monroney (D, OK), chairman of the Senate aviation subcommittee, suggests prohibiting the heirs of suicides in sabotaged planes from collecting insurance as a means of safeguarding commercial airliners.

***March** 26:*   Swedish experts are puzzled over the nation's high suicide rate. Government officials reject efforts to link the rate to the social welfare system.

***May** 11:*   In a report to the American Psychiatric Association, Dr. Robert E. Litman notes most persons with suicidal tendencies show drastic behaviorial changes.

***July** 27:*   President Eisenhower's remark linking the high suicide rate of an unnamed European country to its socialist philosophy is seen as a reference to Sweden. The comment draws a critical reaction in Sweden and other Scandinavian countries. (Jul. 29, '62)

***October** 20:*   A British Criminal Law Revision Commission urges suicide and attempted suicide no longer be held as crimes. (Feb. 28, '58; Oct. 19, '59; Aug. 4, '61)

1961

***May** 8:*   After a patient study, Bellevue Hospital in New York City reports a startling incidence of suicide attempts among children and adolescents.

***July** 2:*   Author Ernest Hemingway kills himself by shotgun blast in his home in Idaho.

***August** 4:*   The British government officially approves legislation removing the offense of suicide from the statute books. It is the first time in 1,000 years suicide is not a crime in Great Britain. Assisting or aiding a suicide remains a criminal offense. (Feb. 28, '58; Oct. 19, '59; Oct. 20, '60)

September 12:   The suicide rate in East Berlin rises sharply following the closing of the West Berlin border.

1962

July 29:   Former President Eisenhower apologizes to Sweden for his 1960 remarks linking the nation's high suicide rate to its socialist philosophy. (Jul. 27, '60)

August 5:   Actress Marilyn Monroe dies from an overdose of sleeping pills.

August 14:   The 12 suicides in New York City set a record for a single day. Marilyn Monroe's death is believed to be a factor.

September 28:   A Church of England committee proposes that people who commit suicide be given church services and burial in consecrated ground.

1963

February 11:   The American poet and novelist Sylvia Plath commits suicide in London.

May 4:   The American Health Institute, reporting on world rates, finds the incidence of suicide among Protestants seven times as high as among Catholics or Jews.

June 11:   A Buddhist monk immolates himself in protest against the government of South Vietnam. The image of a seated figure in flames would become familiar to Americans as Buddhist monks burned themselves to death as a form of protest throughout the Vietnam war.

August 9:   A Public Health Service survey reports tranquilizing drugs now rival barbiturates as suicide pills.

October 25:   A five-year study at Harvard University of traffic deaths concludes that superficial police probes fail to uncover apparent "autocides."

1964

May 4:   The Los Angeles Neuropsychiatric Institute reports that approximately 5 million persons (1 in 40) now living in the United States have attempted suicide.

Chronology

1965

March 20: A report to the American Orthopsychiatric Association notes that teen suicides have doubled in the last ten years while figures for all suicides rose about 50 percent.

April 1: The *Journal of the American Medical Association* reports that the suicide mood appears to be highest on Wednesday nights and lowest on Saturday nights. Suicide is ranked as one of the ten leading causes of death in the United States.

July 24: The Turkish air force initiates a probe into the attempted mass suicides by cadets who failed exams at a service school.

October 14: At a seminar on suicide sponsored by the George Washington University of Medicine, Dr. Stanley F. Yolles, director of the National Institute of Mental Health, discloses plans to establish a national suicide prevention center as part of the institute. (Oct. 24, '66)

1966

February 4: A radio audience in New York City hears a woman threaten suicide during a telephone interview. The woman is placed under medical care after the station alerts police.

April 29: Atlanta announces plans for a suicide prevention service with special phones. Those contemplating suicide can call for counsel.

September 9: Refugees from the People's Republic of China in Hong Kong report the Red Guard youth movement (the Cultural Revolution) has caused a wave of suicides.

October 24: Dr. Edwin S. Shneidman is named the first director of the newly formed Center for the Study of Suicide Prevention at the National Institute of Mental Health. (Oct. 14, '65)

November 24: The World Health Organization reveals plans to provide suicide prevention services.

1967

January 7: Richard J. Paris, who had deserted from his army base, commits suicide by setting off 50 sticks of dynamite in a Las Vegas motel. The blast kills his wife and four others and injures 12.

January 29: An editorial in the *Journal of the American Medical Association* urges doctors to assume a primary role in suicide prevention. The editorial notes many disturbed persons consult their doctor prior to attempting suicide.

March 2: Vatican Radio holds that the maritime tradition that the captain should go down with a sinking ship is suicide and therefore sinful.

April 1: A longtime study of 50,000 college men by the National Heart Institute indicates that the death of a student's father in the precollegiate years predisposes the student to suicide.

May 8: Two surveys of the medical profession find that doctors in general are twice as likely and psychiatrists in particular are four times as likely to commit suicide.

1968

September 6: Dr. Edwin S. Shneidman founds the American Association of Suicidology.

November 19: An Office of Economic Opportunity report highlights the fact that the suicide rate of men over 55 is four times that of younger men. Poverty is identified as a major cause of suicide among older Americans.

1969

March 7: The British House of Lords passes without debate a bill that would allow doctors to comply with the requests of incurable patients to end their lives. The euthanasia measure was subsequently defeated in a second vote.

June 20: In research sponsored by the National Institute of Mental Health, Professor Herbert Hendin finds that the serious suicide problem among young blacks in urban areas is intimately related to the effects of life in inner city slums.

October 5: Diane Linkletter, daughter of TV personality Art Linkletter, commits suicide while under the influence of hallucinatory drugs.

October 16: Two 17-year-old youths commit suicide near Blackwood, New Jersey, after attending a rally protesting the Vietnam war. They leave notes urging peace and brotherhood for mankind.

1970

January 24: In the fifth such suicide in France in a week, a 17-year-old girl immolates herself in Paris. Four more similar suicides occur in the following days and the nation is riven by the apparent epidemic of self-immolations.

February 25: Russian-born American painter Mark Rothko commits suicide in New York City.

October 12:   In a message delivered to a convention of Catholic doctors in Washington, D.C., Pope Paul VI equates euthanasia with abortion and declares that Christianity teaches an absolute respect for man from conception to death.

November 25:   The Japanese writer Yukio Mishima and four followers break into a national defense headquarters in Tokyo. Advocating a return to an imperial Japan, Mishima publicly commits *seppuku.* (Nov. 25, '80)

1971

March 3:   A special Committee for Reform of Canon Law suggests the Roman Catholic Church lift its ban on religious burials for suicides, heretics, and Freemasons.

1972

January 7:   John Berryman, one of America's leading poets, jumps to his death from a bridge over the Mississippi River.

April 2:   Data concerning the increase in suicide among the young, and young women in particular, are presented at the annual convention of the American Association of Suicidology.

April 16:   Nobel Prize–winning novelist Yasunari Kawabata commits suicide in his native Japan.

June 3:   Pope Paul VI urges participants at an International College of Surgeons convention to help the church defend Christian ethics against the "hedonism" of contraceptives, abortion, and euthanasia.

August 7:   Medical experts, testifying at hearings on "Death with Dignity" held by a Special Senate Committee on Aging, disagree on whether terminally ill or injured patients have a right to euthanasia.

1973

January 27:   Michael James Brody, Jr., the millionaire heir who drew headlines in 1970 when he announced he would give away his fortune, kills himself with a hunting rifle at a relative's home in New York.

May 24:   Representative William O. Mills (R, Md), whose 1971 election was aided by an unreported transfer of $25,000 from President Nixon's campaign committee, is found shot to death. Authorities term his death an apparent suicide.

August 1:   A Gallup Poll reveals that 53% of Americans interviewed favor mercy killing for people with incurable diseases if requested by the patient and family. Only 36% said they approved of such a practice in a similar poll taken in 1950. The greatest change in views occurred in adults under age 30.

September 11: Salvador Allende, president of Chile, dies during a military coup that overthrows his government. Allende apparently committed suicide, although many supporters maintained he was murdered.

October 14: William A. Rockefeller, a scion of the family famed for its wealth and power, dies of a self-inflicted shotgun wound.

December 4: The American Medical Association reiterates its opposition to mercy killing, but concurs that a person dying of an incurable disease should be able to refuse extraordinary life-sustaining measures.

1974

January 5: ABC's *Close-Up* series broadcasts "The Right to Die." The documentary addresses the ability of medical science to prolong human life and the impact this is having on the question of death and dying.

January 16: A survey by *Medical Opinion* magazine finds that the acceptance of euthanasia has become widespread in the medical profession. Of the doctors canvassed, 79% agreed that people have the right to make their wishes concerning passive euthanasia known before serious illness strikes.

October 4: Critically acclaimed poet Anne Sexton commits suicide. She had been a close friend of poet Sylvia Plath, who had killed herself in 1963.

1975

January 28: Dr. and Mrs. Henry P. Van Dusen, long advocates of euthanasia, swallow an overdose of sleeping pills in carrying out a suicide pact at their Princeton, New Jersey, home. Mrs. Van Dusen died immediately and Dr. Van Dusen, a leading theologian, died 15 days later. The elderly couple's suicide generated considerable interest and debate.

February 3: Eli M. Black, chairman of the United Brands Company, jumps to his death from the Pan Am Building in New York City.

April 10: James W. Howe, husband of First Lady Betty Ford's personal secretary, commits suicide. His death sets off a federal probe that leads to the investigation into South Korean efforts to illegally influence congressional policy (Koreagate).

May 4: A recent Gallup Poll indicates that 51% of Americans believe it is morally wrong to commit suicide. Of those interviewed, 53% maintain that individuals with incurable diseases do not have the moral right to end their lives; 40% condone the practice.

June 18:   Mason J. Condon, a district engineer in Massachusetts, dies after shooting himself in the head in front of the jury that convicted him of extorting monies from companies doing business with the state.

June 19:   A Cornell University study reports that suicides among those aged 15 to 19 have tripled in the last two decades.

October 24:   More than 500 experts from 21 nations assembled in Jerusalem for the Eighth International Congress on Suicide Prevention debate the moral and medical issues raised by suicide.

December 6:   Advice columnist Abigail Van Buren receives a special award at the annual conference of the Euthanasia Education Council in New York City for her efforts in publicizing the living will.

1976

March 31:   In a landmark decision, the New Jersey Supreme Court rules **In re Quinlan** that the parents of Karen Ann Quinlan may disconnect the respirator keeping their comatose daughter alive. (Jun. 11, '85)

April 9:   Folk singer Phil Ochs kills himself at age 35.

April 14:   James W. Tilson, head of the Immigration and Naturalization Service, is found dead of a self-inflicted gunshot wound.

September 17:   California enacts the nation's first Natural Death Act.

October 1:   In the October issue of the *Archives of General Psychiatry*, Dr. Marie Asberg reports the findings of her team at the Karolinska Institute in Stockholm that there is a link between low levels of the brain chemical serotonin and clinical depression. (Jun. 1, '81)

November 15:   Convicted murderer Gary Mark Gilmore, in a Utah state prison cell, and his girlfriend, Nicole Barret, in her apartment in Provo, each take an overdose of barbiturates in an apparent suicide pact. Both survive the attempted suicide and Gilmore is subsequently executed in January 1977.

December 15:   A Canadian Jesuit priest, recently expelled from Vietnam after 18 years of missionary work there, claims 15,000 to 20,000 Vietnamese have committed suicide since the fall of South Vietnam to communism the previous year.

1977

January 28:   Actor Freddie Prinze fatally wounds himself with a gunshot to the temple. His suicide stuns his friends and fans.

May 17: Writer James A. Wechsler discusses his son Michael's suicide in his newspaper column in the *New York Post.*

August 3: The President's Commission on Mental Health notes that the suicide rate among elderly women is increasing.

August 24: A TV documentary in which a hidden police camera records a woman urging her mother to commit suicide airs in Great Britain. The woman was later convicted of aiding and abetting an attempted suicide and was jailed for two years. The case touched off widespread controversy not only about the actual incident but also about the right to privacy and ethics in TV and criminal justice.

December 31: By the end of the year, seven states have followed California's lead in enacting living will laws.

1978

July 1: The National Right to Life Committee at its convention in St. Louis opens a drive for a constitutional amendment to bar euthanasia.

July 18: British authorities announce they will not prosecute Derek Humphry for the role he had played in his wife's suicide three years earlier. Humphry had described how he had helped his wife Jean, suffering from incurable cancer, end her own life in his book *Jean's Way.*

October 3: In the first right-to-die case involving a competent patient, a Florida district court of appeals holds in **Satz v. Perlmutter** that an elderly man suffering from Lou Gehrig's disease has the right to have the respirator that is keeping him alive disconnected.

October 19: Actor Gig Young kills his wife of three weeks and then shoots himself in a murder-suicide.

November 18: The Reverend Jim Jones leads over 900 members of his People's Temple cult in a mass suicide-execution at Jonestown in the South American nation of Guyana. The event was triggered by the visit of Congressman Leo J. Ryan (D, CA) who was investigating the mistreatment of Jones's American followers. Ryan and three others in his party were killed by cult members. News of the mass suicide shocked the world.

1979

June 10: Artist Jo Roman, long an advocate of "self-termination," deliberately takes an overdose of Seconal in her apartment in New York City. She left a statement, a manuscript, and 19 hours of videotape in which she explained and defended her suicide. (Jun. 16, '80)

September 4: A California Court of Appeals rules that an insane person "cannot form the intent to take his own life." The ruling, seen as affecting numerous insurance policies, came in a suit by a widow against an insurance company that refused to pay her claim on an insurance policy taken by her late husband ten months before he committed suicide.

1980

March 31: The film *Ordinary People*, which portrays the struggle of a family to deal with death and suicide, wins the Academy Award as best picture for 1980.

June 16: A controversial hour-long documentary on the suicide of artist Jo Roman is broadcast on public television. "Choosing Suicide" traces the decision of the 62-year-old woman, diagnosed as having breast cancer, to deliberately end her own life. (Jun. 10, '79)

June 26: The Roman Catholic Church reaffirms its condemnation of euthanasia, but states that individuals in certain circumstances have the right to renounce extraordinary and burdensome life-support systems available to dying patients in modern hospitals.

August 11: The British euthanasia group Exit cancels plans to publish a guide on how to commit suicide after being advised the publication might result in prosecution.

August 15: The Hemlock Society, a new California-based organization dedicated to the right of terminally ill people to "self-deliverance," reveals its plan to publish a guide to suicide. The announcement came after the British euthanasia group Exit abandoned plans for a similar publication.

September 3: Television talk-show host Phil Donahue conducts a two-part program on college student suicides as part of NBC's *Today Show*. The idea was to highlight the growing problem of youth suicide.

November 25: About 1,300 people in Tokyo observe the tenth anniversary of the suicide of writer Yukio Mishima. (Nov. 25, '70)

1981

January 19: Former heavyweight boxing champion Muhammad Ali talks an unidentified young man out of jumping from a nine-story building in Los Angeles.

March 31: New York State's highest court rules in the case of Brother Joseph Fox, a member of a Roman Catholic order, that life-sustaining procedures may be terminated for patients who are fatally ill and also have given "clear and convincing evidence" they do not wish to be kept alive through artificial means.

May 5: Irish Republican Army hunger striker Bobby Sands dies after a 66-day fast in a Belfast prison. Sands, whose suicidal protest drew worldwide attention, sought unsuccessfully to gain political status for imprisoned IRA guerillas.

May 19: The American Medical Association and the American Psychiatric Association jointly undertake a new study of suicide among doctors as part of a nationwide effort to prevent self-destructive behavior among physicians.

June 1: A joint team from the National Institute of Mental Health and the Karolinska Institute in Stockholm announce in the June issue of *Archives of General Psychiatry* that they have isolated a "suicide factor," the chemical serotonin found in the brain. Especially low levels of the neurotransmitter were found in suicidal persons. (Oct. 1, '76)

July 9: The President's Commission for the Study of Ethical Problems in Medicine and Biomedical and Behavioral Research, established by Congress in 1978, recommends that death be defined as the "irreversible cessation" of all brain functions. The commission urges adoption by all the states of a proposed Uniform Determination of Death Act. (Jan. 7, '82; Mar. 21, '83)

October 21: Psychiatrist Dr. Thomas Radecki testifies before a congressional committee investigating television violence that the 1981 film *The Deerhunter* had inspired 27 cases of persons with self-inflicted wounds who had imitated the Russian roulette scenes in the movie.

November 21: Chicago officials report that two male viewers had fatally shot themselves playing Russian roulette after viewing the film *The Deerhunter* on television.

December 10: The Metromedia presentation "Teenage Suicide: Don't Try It" is broadcast. Narrated by Timothy Hutton, who portrayed a suicidal youth in the award-winning film *Ordinary People*, the TV program addresses what it terms an epidemic of teen suicide.

December 13: "In Loveland: Study of a Teenage Suicide" airs on the ABC News *Directions* series.

December 29: A report in the publication *Archives of General Psychiatry* finds that "holiday syndrome," thought to increase the number of suicide attempts, is not as widespread or serious as previously believed.

1982

January 7: The Presidential Commission on Ethical Problems in Medicine and Biomedical and Behavioral Research approves guidelines that say it is morally acceptable in certain cases to terminate extraordinary treatment measures for permanently unconscious patients. (Jul. 9, '81; Mar. 21, '83)

February 1: The body of wildlife photographer Carl McCunn is recovered in the Alaskan wilderness. A diary found with the body described how McCunn decided to shoot himself as he ran out of food and hope in the frozen terrain.

February 9: A National Center for Health Statistics report shows striking differences in suicide rates for various ethnic groups in the United States.

July 4: The former president of the Dominican Republic, Silvestre Antonio Guzman Fernandez, dies from a self-inflicted gunshot wound.

September 13: Leicester C. Hemingway, a writer and only brother of the late novelist Ernest Hemingway, fatally shoots himself.

October 28: The Society for the Right to Die sponsors a meeting in Boston of ten distinguished physicians with the purpose of formulating guidelines for the care of hopelessly ill patients. The results of the meeting were published in an influential article, "The Physician's Responsibility Toward Hopelessly Ill Patients," in the *New England Journal of Medicine* in April 1984. (Mar. 30, '89)

1983

January 31: The Health and Human Services Department reports that accidents, murders, and suicides are responsible for three out of four deaths among people 15 to 24 years old.

March 3: Writer Arthur Koestler and his wife are found dead after committing suicide in London.

March 4: After calling TV station WHMA to inform it of his plans, Cecil Andrews, an unemployed roofer, attempts to immolate himself in the Jacksonville, Alabama, town square to protest unemployment in the United States. Two cameramen from the station filmed the entire 82-second incident, with one cameraman making an effort to put the fire out only after 37 seconds had elapsed. The failure of the cameramen to intervene in the unsuccessful suicide attempt drew widespread condemnation.

March 21: The Presidential Commission on Ethical Problems in Medicine and Biomedical and Behavioral Research endorses providing pain-relieving drugs for hopelessly ill patients in unbearable pain, even if the drugs may hasten the moment of death. (Jul. 9, '81; Jan. 7, '82)

April 29: The first National Voluntary Euthanasia Conference is held in San Francisco.

September 20: The Veterans Administration amends its rules to allow its doctors, at the request of a dying patient, to bar resuscitation or extraordinary life-saving measures.

October 23: Suicide bombers drive trucks loaded with explosives into U.S. and French military compounds in Beirut, Lebanon. In the attack, 241 American marines are killed. The tactic of suicide bombings comes to symbolize the fanaticism of Islamic fundamentalism.

1984

March 18: A series of teenage suicides in the northern suburbs of New York City will be examined as part of a four-year study by a Columbia University psychiatric team.

August 27: The shocked community of Marina, California, sends food and money to the family of 13-year-old Danny Holley, who hanged himself after telling his mother "if there was one less mouth to feed, things would be better."

September 12: In a guest editorial in *The New York Times*, Alfred B. DelBello, head of the National Committee on Youth Suicide Prevention, calls for the establishment of a national commission on youth suicide.

September 19: A number of well-known French doctors, in an unusual public declaration, reveal that they have helped some of their terminally ill patients to die.

September 22: An international convention of Associations for the Right to Die in Dignity is held in Nice, France.

September 23: In a *New York Times*/CBS News Poll, 77% of the respondents agree that the terminally ill should be allowed to request that life-sustaining measures be withdrawn.

October 3: A Senate Judiciary Juvenile Justice Subcommittee holds hearings on the rise in teenage suicide.

October 13: A team of psychologists conducts counseling sessions with students at Clear Lake High School, Houston, after the suicides of six teenagers in the last two and a half months.

October 16: *Hear Me Cry*, a drama about two high school sophomores who form a suicide pact, is broadcast as a CBS Schoolbreak Special. In conjunction with the broadcast of the film and another movie to be shown later in the month, the network distributes educational materials to schools.

October 25:   The body of counterculture poet and writer Richard Brautigan is found in California. The cause of death was a self-inflicted gunshot wound.

October 30:   The television movie *Silence of the Heart* airs on CBS. The film depicts the surviving family of a teenage suicide.

November 1:   Students at Colorado University vote against having the school look into the possibility of stockpiling cyanide capsules for use in the event of nuclear war.

December 14:   Experts at a conference of the National Committee on Youth Suicide Prevention recommend the development and introduction of programs to prevent teenage suicides into U.S. high schools.

December 27:   In a case that drew nationwide attention to right-to-die issues, a California appeals court rules in **Bartling v. Superior Court** that a man suffering from five fatal diseases had a right to refuse medical treatment.

1985

January 17:   In its decision in **In re Conroy,** the New Jersey Supreme Court holds that all life-sustaining treatment can be withheld or withdrawn from terminally ill patients who so desire.

February 10:   ABC airs a three-hour movie, *Surviving*, about the suicide of two teenagers and its impact on their parents.

February 28:   It is revealed that Marguerite Liegeois, the 73-year-old founding member of France's Association for the Right to Die with Dignity, killed herself the previous week after sending a letter to association members explaining her decision to end her own life due to declining health.

March 4:   In the first federal court ruling in a right-to-die case, the U.S. District Court for the District of Columbia authorizes the cessation of life-support measures for a terminally ill woman in **Tune v. Walter Reed Army Medical Hospital.**

April 1:   Jeanne Deckers, the guitar-playing "Singing Nun" who won worldwide fame, is found dead after committing suicide at her home in Belgium.

May 1:   Secretary of Health and Human Services Margaret M. Heckler directs the establishment in May 1985 of a department-wide Task Force on Youth Suicide to examine the problem of youth suicide and propose measures for its prevention. (Aug. 1, '85; Oct. 1, '87)

June 1:   June 1985 is proclaimed "Youth Suicide Prevention Month" by President Ronald Reagan.

The Youth Suicide National Center is established as a nonprofit educational organization in Washington, D.C. The same month the center cosponsors with the Department of Health and Human Services a two-day National Conference on Youth Suicide.

June 11: Karen Ann Quinlan dies of respiratory failure in a New Jersey nursing home. (Mar. 31, '76)

August 1: The Secretary's Task Force on Youth Suicide begins its work in August 1985 under the direction of chairman Dr. Shervert H. Frazier. (May 1, '85; Oct. 1, '87)

August 9: The August 1985 National Conference of Commissioners on Uniform State Laws approves a draft Uniform Rights of the Terminally Ill Act. The draft law is recommended for enactment in all the states.

August 25: The head of TSR Hobbies rejects assertions that the company's game Dungeons and Dragons leads some teenagers to suicide.

October 1: Former Senator Jacob K. Javits (R, NY), himself fatally ill, testifies before a House Select Committee on Aging in favor of legislation that would allow terminally ill persons to make living wills and to "die with dignity."

October 21: Dan White, convicted of fatally shooting San Francisco Mayor George Moscone in 1978, commits suicide.

1986

February 8: The third student in a week from the same high school commits suicide in Omaha, Nebraska.

March 13: Former Queens Borough President Donald R. Manes stabs himself to death in the kitchen of his home. Manes, who had attempted suicide in January, resigned from his New York City post the previous month over allegations of corruption.

March 15: The Council on Ethical and Judicial Affairs of the American Medical Association issues a majority opinion that it is ethical for doctors to withhold "all means of life prolonging treatment," including food and water, from patients in irreversible comas even if death is not imminent.

April 18: Ruling in *Corbett v. D'Alessandro*, a Florida district court of appeals determines that patients in a permanent vegetative state who had previously indicated their desire not to be kept alive through artificial means had a right to reject artificial feeding.

May 23: A Metropolitan Life Insurance Company report finds that persons aged 15 to 44 now account for the majority of U.S. suicides.

June 5:   A California court of appeals upholds the right of Elizabeth Bouvia to refuse nourishment of any kind in **Bouvia v. Superior Court.**

June 29:   U.S. Senator John P. East (R, NC) is found dead on the floor of his garage. East, who had announced he would not seek reelection due to ill health, had asphyxiated from breathing carbon monoxide. The death was ruled a suicide.

August 7:   A Los Angeles superior court throws out a lawsuit against rock star Ozzie Osbourne and CBS Records which charged that the British singer's music contributed to the suicide of a teenager in 1984. The suit was brought by the parents of a 19-year-old who shot himself after listening to Osbourne's recordings.

August 20:   Patrick Henry Sherril, a mail carrier facing problems at work, opens fire in a post office in Edmond, Oklahoma. He kills 14 postal workers and wounds seven others before taking his own life with a bullet in the head.

August 22:   The *New England Journal of Medicine* publishes recommended guidelines for the treatment of hopelessly ill patients.

August 29:   A woman suffering from an inoperable and malignant brain tumor is authorized by a Virginia court to halt her artificial feeding. The case, *Hazelton v. Powhaton Nursing Home*, was the first instance of a court interpreting the language of a natural death act.

September 10:   A study published in the *New England Journal of Medicine* suggests that television news coverage of suicides and television dramas about the topic appear to cause a temporary increase in the number of teenage suicides. (Sep. 24, '87)

September 11:   The Massachusetts Supreme Judicial Court holds in **Brophy v. New England Sinai Hospital** that the family of a comatose man may have his feeding tube disconnected so he can die.

November 28:   A poll published by the American Medical Association shows that 73% of Americans surveyed support withdrawing life support under certain conditions from patients with no real chance of recovery.

1987

January 21:   The American Suicide Foundation, dedicated to suicide prevention through research and education, is established in New York City.

January 22:   At a news conference in his office in Harrisburg, Pennsylvania state treasurer R. Budd Dwyer fatally shoots himself. The major networks do not show the graphic footage but report the incident.

Suicide

A Colorado district court rules in **In re Rodas** that a mentally alert 34-year-old man who was severely paralyzed and impaired could refuse life-sustaining artificial nutrition and hydration.

February 9: Former National Security Advisor Robert C. McFarlane, distraught at the unfolding Iran-contra scandal, unsuccessfully attempts to commit suicide with an overdose of Valium.

March 11: Four teenagers are found dead of carbon monoxide poisoning in a car parked in a Bergenfield, New Jersey, garage, along with a suicide note asking they be waked and buried together. Their suicide pact shocks the nation and leads to widespread appeals for further efforts to prevent youth suicide.

A 14-year-old boy kills himself in the garage of his home in the Chicago suburb of Rolling Meadows. Newspaper clippings on six recent teenage suicides are found in his bedroom.

March 13: Two young women are found dead in a garage full of auto exhaust in Alsip, Illinois. The teenagers each had left a suicide note.

March 17: Two more youths try to commit suicide in the same Bergenfield, New Jersey, garage where four teenagers asphyxiated themselves March 11. Their unsuccessful attempt came hours after the suicide of a young man who was found dead in a running car in his family's garage in the nearby town of Clifton.

March 30: The Center for Demographic Studies at Duke University reports that suicide is increasing among the elderly.

June 1: In *Delio v. Westchester County Medical Center*, a New York appeals court authorizes the cessation of tube feeding for patients in a persistent vegetative state.

June 4: The Joint Commission on Accreditation of Hospitals, the main agency that accredits hospitals in the United States, announces that as of January 1988 all accredited hospitals must have established policies on withholding resuscitation from terminally ill patients. A study by the commission indicated that 40% of the nation's hospitals did not have such formal guidelines.

June 24: The New Jersey Supreme Court issues three major right-to-die decisions that affirm the rights of patients to refuse medical treatments.

June 26: It is announced that a procedure for detecting a person's predisposition to commit suicide has been patented by a Connecticut doctor. The human voice is to be used in diagnosing and treating suicidal behavior.

Chronology

July 27: In a case that drew wide attention because the patient, Tom Wirth, had AIDS, a New York Court refuses to order the cessation of the treatment that was keeping him alive because there was a remote chance his condition might improve. Wirth died shortly thereafter.

July 29: Hungary, worried by the highest recorded suicide rate in the world, encourages extensive study of its causes as part of an effort to find ways of prevention.

July 31: A study by the congressional research agency, the Office of Technology Assessment, reports that the terminally ill are often left out of treatment decisions. The study urges the greater use of living wills.

August 17: Nazi war criminal Rudolf Hess, after several previously unsuccessful attempts, commits suicide in Spandau Prison in Berlin.

August 19: A Pennsylvania court of common pleas grants the request of a dying woman to have the respirator keeping her alive disconnected.

September 14: Pope John Paul II, speaking to Roman Catholic health care workers in Phoenix, reiterates the church's steadfast rejection of euthanasia.

September 24: The *New England Journal of Medicine* reports that researchers in California were unable to duplicate a widely publicized study that found suicide increases among teenagers when it is depicted on television. (Sep. 10, '86)

October 1: The Task Force on Youth Suicide concludes its study into the causes of the high suicide rate among the young. Chairman Dr. Shervert H. Frazier submits detailed recommendations on youth suicide prevention to Health and Human Services Secretary Otis R. Bowen. (May 1, '85; Aug. 1, '85)

December 3: The Maine Supreme Judicial Court upholds the right of persons in a persistent vegetative state to have artificial means of feeding withdrawn.

December 15: A Michigan county court endorses the right of a terminally ill patient to request the cessation of all life-sustaining procedures.

1988

January 8: In an anonymous essay entitled "It's Over, Debbie" in the *Journal of the American Medical Association,* a resident physician describes administering a lethal dose of morphine to a young woman dying of cancer. The essay sparks controversy in the medical community with many condemning the doctor's actions. Citing First Amendment press freedoms, the AMA refuses to disclose the author's name to the Illinois

State Attorney's office, which is considering possible prosecution for murder.

March 18: A Cook County circuit court dismisses the Illinois state attorney's request for the American Medical Association to divulge the name of the doctor who wrote an anonymous account of killing a terminally ill cancer patient. The court ruled there was insufficient evidence that a crime had been committed.

March 31: Of the approximately 2,000 adult Americans surveyed by the Roper Organization for the Hemlock Society, 58% agree that it should be lawful for a physician to end the life of a terminally ill patient at the patient's request.

May 9: Supporters of a measure that would allow terminally ill patients to request a lethal injection from a physician fail to gather enough signatures to place the issue on the November ballot in California.

May 13: Findings presented at the annual conference of the American Psychiatric Association indicate there are chemical abnormalities in the brains of depressed teenagers that appear to predispose them to suicide.

July 22: Carter Vanderbilt Cooper, 23, son of fashion designer and heiress Gloria Vanderbilt, jumps to his death from his mother's Manhattan apartment.

August 29: The Federal Centers for Disease Control in Atlanta issues a report containing guidelines and recommendations to help communities prevent clusters of suicides, particularly among the young.

November 16: The Missouri Supreme Court, in **Cruzan v. Harmon,** bars the family of a comatose woman from taking any actions that would permit her to die. (Jul. 3, '89)

1989

January 31: The Connecticut Supreme Court affirms that the state's Removal of Life Support Systems Act permits the withholding or withdrawing of tube feeding.

March 30: The results of a second meeting of prominent physicians convened by the Society for the Right to Die are published in the "Physician's Responsibility Toward Hopelessly Ill Patients—A Second Look" in the *New England Journal of Medicine.* The article addresses the obligation of health care professionals to respect the right of terminally ill patients to decide the nature of the care they receive. (Oct. 28, '82)

April 12: Abbie Hoffman, social activist and a leading figure in the counterculture movement of the 1960s, commits suicide in New Hope, Pennsylvania.

Chronology

April 19: An explosion in a gun turret aboard the battleship USS *Iowa* kills 47 sailors. A highly controversial navy investigation subsequently rules the fatal blast was caused by a suicidal crewmember.

July 3: The U.S. Supreme Court agrees to review the decision in **Cruzan v. Harmon.** It is the first time the nation's highest court has accepted a right-to-die case. (Nov. 16, '88)

October 11: Mark Henry Whalen fatally shoots himself after he and a female companion are apprehended by police in Cape May, New Jersey. The two teenagers from Connecticut stole three powerboats as they worked their way down the Atlantic Coast to their ultimate goal of Florida.

November 21: The Georgia Supreme Court rules that Larry McAfee, paralyzed and unable to breathe on his own, has a constitutional right to withdraw the respirator that has kept him alive for four years.

CHAPTER 3

COURT CASES

In 1976 the New Jersey Supreme Court ruled that the parents of a comatose woman could disconnect the respirator that was keeping her alive. The *Quinlan* decision marked the first time a court had addressed the difficult question of an individual's right to die. In succeeding years courts across the nation would find themselves confronting a range of troubling right-to-die issues. Does a terminally ill person have a right to refuse medical treatment, or is this tantamount to committing suicide? If there is a right to die with dignity, should it extend to severely impaired individuals who are being kept alive through modern medical technology but who, strictly speaking, are not terminally ill? In generally countenancing the right to die, the courts have struggled to define the thin line between allowing persons to end their own lives through the termination of artificial life-sustaining measures and society taking an active role in euthanasia.

This chapter summarizes what are generally considered the most significant right-to-die cases to date. The great majority of such decisions have been handed down in state courts. Although rulings in one state are not automatically binding in another, the cases in this chapter established precedents or involved legal arguments that had an impact on the judicial system nationwide. Each case is presented in the same format: "Background," "Legal Issues," "Decision," and "Impact." Court cases in bold print are discussed separately within the chapter.

IN RE QUINLAN (1976)

Background

Karen Ann Quinlan was 21 when she lapsed into a severe coma in April 1975 following a birthday party for a friend. The exact cause of her coma was never conclusively determined, although doctors believed it stemmed from a combination of alcohol, aspirin, and a prescription tranquilizer. After several months she was diagnosed as being in a persistent vegetative state with no chance of recovery. Her breathing was sustained by a mechanical respirator.

Quinlan's parents believed their daughter was suffering needlessly. They asked a New Jersey Superior Court to designate her father, Joseph Quinlan, as her guardian with authority to direct the "discontinuance of all extraordinary procedures" that were keeping her alive. The Superior Court denied the request and Joseph Quinlan appealed to the New Jersey Supreme Court.

Legal Issues

The lower court had argued that decisions over life-sustaining procedures should be left to the medical profession. It noted that the state had a basic interest in the preservation of life, which took precedence over individual rights concerning medical decisions.

The Quinlans contended that the right to privacy embedded in the U.S. Constitution extended to the right of individuals to determine and control their own medical treatment. They recounted how their daughter previously had expressed the wish never to be kept alive by elaborate artificial means. Consequently the courts should defer to her constitutional right to have the life-support equipment disconnected.

In addition to the privacy right, the Quinlans advanced two other constitutional arguments for authorizing removal of the respirator: first, that the free exercise of religion guaranteed in the First Amendment meant the state should not interfere in personal decisions concerning life and death; second, that the pain their daughter purportedly endured as a result of the respirator should not be allowed under the Eighth Amendment's ban on cruel and unusual punishment.

Decision

In a landmark decision announced March 31, 1976, the New Jersey Supreme Court granted the Quinlans' request, ruling that the "termination of treatment pursuant to the right of privacy is, within the limitations of this case, *ipso facto* lawful." The state's interest in preserving life was counterbalanced by Karen Quinlan's right to privacy and the dim prognosis for her recovery or return to a meaningful existence. The usurpation of her right to privacy through intrusive medical procedures could not be justified because "ultimately there comes a point at which the individual's rights overcome the State interest." Having decided on the basis of the privacy right, the court dismissed the Quinlans' other constitutional arguments as inapplicable.

Joseph Quinlan was appointed his daughter's guardian. The court held that if the immediate family, attending physicians, and hospital ethics committee all concurred, he could direct the withdrawal of Karen Quinlan's life-support apparatus "without any civil or criminal liability . . . on the part of any participant." Death "would not be homicide, but rather expiration from natural causes."

Impact

The *Quinlan* case was significant for two reasons. It was the first case in the nation to address the emerging issue of the right to die. In the 15 years following *Quinlan*, right-to-die cases were litigated in courtrooms across the country. The legal reasoning in *Quinlan* became an important precedent. The case represented the first time a court had identified the constitutional right of privacy as the basis for the right of persons to determine the nature and extent of their medical care. The *Quinlan* ruling was limited to the question of whether extraordinary life-sustaining measures could be withheld or withdrawn from a terminally ill patient. Subsequent decisions would expand on the principle that individuals had a major say in dictating the course of their treatment.

Karen Quinlan was removed from the respirator in May 1976. She unexpectedly began breathing on her own and survived another nine years. She died in June 1985 without ever regaining consciousness.

SATZ V. PERLMUTTER (1978)

Background

Abe Perlmutter, 73, was confined to bed in a Florida hospital. He was dying from amyotrophic lateral sclerosis, or Lou Gehrig's disease, and a mechanical respirator had been attached to his throat to allow him to breathe. Although he had difficulty speaking, Perlmutter was fully conscious and competent. He had told his family of his desire to end his intense suffering. At one point he had attempted to remove the respirator himself, but an alarm sounded and it was reattached.

Perlmutter petitioned the county circuit court to have the respirator disconnected. The trial judge conducted a bedside hearing, after which he authorized the withdrawal of the life-sustaining device. The actual removal of the machine was delayed when the state attorney general appealed the decision to a state appeals court.

Legal Issues

The attorney general contended that removal of the respirator would constitute "self murder." The state had a compelling interest in preventing suicide, even under the circumstances faced by the dying patient in the case at issue. Furthermore, it was asserted that anyone who assisted in disconnecting the respirator would be guilty of aiding a suicide.

Perlmutter claimed his constitutional right to privacy encompassed the right to refuse medical treatment and noted that the common law had long recognized persons as the masters of their own bodies. This mastery extended to the right to prohibit even life-saving procedures or measures. Perlmutter's counsel argued that removal of the respirator could not be construed as suicide because the underlying cause of death would be his terminal medical condition. He was not committing suicide but choosing to die with dignity.

Decision

The District Court of Appeal ruled in favor of Perlmutter. In a decision handed down on October 3, 1978, the court found no reason to force Perlmutter to live, against his expressed will, while "inflicting never-ending physical torture on his body until the inevitable, but artificially suspended, moment of death." The state's contention of "self murder" was rejected because Perlmutter's illness was not self-inflicted. This illness would be the ultimate cause of death were his respirator disconnected. Taking into account that the patient's family was in agreement with the decision and the "exigencies" of the situation, the appeals court did not forward the case to the Florida Supreme Court for review.

Impact

Perlmutter's family gathered at his bedside the day after the ruling. The respirator was withdrawn and he died 40 hours later.

The state attorney general then applied to the Florida Supreme Court for review with the intent of having the court clarify the law on right-to-die questions. The Supreme Court unanimously upheld the *Perlmutter* opinion but declined to establish guidelines for future cases. The state's highest court stated that right-to-die issues should more properly be addressed through legislation. This occurred in 1984 when the state legislature enacted the Florida Life-Prolonging Procedure Act.

As the nation's first right-to-die case involving the fully aware and competent patient, *Perlmutter* became an important precedent for similar cases in other states. But it is important to note that Perlmutter suffered from a fatal illness. The courts still are struggling with the question of whether to allow persons with severe medical problems who are not terminally ill to halt life-sustaining treatments.

BARTLING V. SUPERIOR COURT (1984)

Background

William F. Bartling had been in poor health for six years when he was admitted to the Glendale Adventist Medical Center in April 1984. The 70-year-old California resident suffered from emphysema, arteriosclerosis, a malignant lung tumor, chronic respiratory failure, and an abdominal aneurysm. Each of the five medical conditions is normally fatal. One of his lungs collapsed during treatment and he was placed on a respirator.

Bartling attempted to withdraw the device several times, and his wrists were placed in restraints. The hospital and his attending physicians refused repeated requests from both the patient and his wife to have the respirator and restraints removed. In June Bartling turned to a state superior court for an injunction to stop the hospital and physicians from administering further treatment without his consent. The hospital contested his request.

The trial court found that Bartling was legally competent and that his diseases had not progressed to the point where he could be considered terminally ill. Interpreting California's Natural Death Act to limit the right to have life-support measures discontinued to comatose, terminally ill patients, the court denied Bartling's petition. Disconnecting the respirator, the court noted, would amount to aiding a suicide or even a homicide.

Bartling appealed the decision. He died on November 6, one day before a California court of appeals was scheduled to hear his case. The court went ahead with the hearing because of the important issues involved.

Legal Issues

The Glendale Adventist Medical Center maintained that it would be a violation of medical ethics to turn off Bartling's respirator. The hospital's responsibility was to preserve life, not hasten its end. In addition, allowing Bartling to die raised questions of possible civil or criminal liability.

Bartling had sought to resolve the issue of liability. He had signed documents releasing the hospital and doctors from responsibility for the removal of life-support equipment. He had also prepared a living will and a declaration in which he stated he did not want to live under his current circumstances. In a videotaped deposition, he had indicated that he had no desire to die but did not want to live on the respirator.

Bartling's counsel argued that the constitutional right to privacy protected an individual's right to refuse medical treatment. It did not matter if the patient was comatose or terminally ill or not. The respirator inserted in Bartling's throat had constituted an intrusive and unwarranted invasion of his body and privacy.

Decision

The Court of Appeals issued its decision on December 27, 1984. Siding clearly with Bartling, the court held that the right to refuse medical treatment was rooted in both the federal and California constitutions. This right "predated the Natural Death Act" and could not be denied to a "competent adult patient."

The court left no doubt about the individual's primacy in decisions concerning health care. "If the right of the patient to self-determination as to his own medical treatment is to have any meaning at all, it must be paramount to the interests of the patient's hospital and doctors. The right of a competent adult patient to refuse medical treatment is a constitutionally guaranteed right which must not be abridged."

Bartling's written statements were cited as clear evidence of his desire to have the respirator withdrawn. The hospital and physicians were required to comply with his instructions. There was no potential liability involved because (1) the refusal of medical treatment was not equatable to suicide and (2) acceding to a patient's legal request to terminate treatment was neither homicide nor euthanasia. If the patient expired after life-sustaining measures were removed, the cause of death would be the underlying medical condition.

Impact

The *Bartling* case drew nationwide attention. Bartling's devastating medical condition earned him much sympathy and support. Although he suffered from a series of potentially fatal diseases, he was not yet technically terminally ill. None of his ailments had advanced to the point where it was a pending, immediate cause of death. Bartling's death while his case was on appeal did not change the fact that the court considered him a nonterminal patient when reaching its decision. As such, *Bartling* represented the first instance in which a court authorized the termination of life-support measures for a competent person who was not near death.

IN RE CONROY (1985)

Background

Claire Conroy was 84 and a resident of a New Jersey nursing home. She suffered from a serious illness and was expected to die within a year. Her ability to swallow was severely limited, and a nasogastric feeding tube had been inserted to supply her with nutrients and fluids. Although not in a coma, she was incompetent or unable to understand or make decisions concerning her own medical care.

Thomas Whittemore, Conroy's nephew, had been appointed her guardian. Believing his aunt would not have wanted the feeding tube inserted, he petitioned the state courts in 1982 to have it removed. The trial court approved Whitemore's request in early 1983. The court reasoned that Conroy's life had become permanently burdensome and that to prolong it was pointless and cruel.

The court had appointed a guardian *ad litem*, or legal guardian, to serve as a disinterested protector of Conroy's interests during the proceedings. The guardian *ad litem* appealed the trial court's decision and the order to remove the feeding tube was stayed. Shortly thereafter, on February 15, 1983, Conroy died. Her death made the appeal moot, but the appellate division of the State Supreme Court went ahead with the case because of its ramifications.

The appeals court subsequently reversed the trial court's judgment. The court found that removing Conroy's feeding tube would have "constituted homicide" in violation of the basic medical principle to "do no harm." Whittemore then appealed to the New Jersey Supreme Court.

Legal Issues

In re Conroy presented several new right-to-die legal issues. In 1976 in **Quinlan** the New Jersey Supreme Court ruled that the parents of a comatose women in a persistent vegetative state could disconnect the respirator that allowed her to breathe. Courts in other states had extended the right to terminate life-sustaining medical procedures to terminally ill patients who were competent and able to make their own decisions concerning life and death. In all these cases the life-prolonging measures to be withdrawn were machines or devices such as a respirator.

Clarie Conroy was neither comatose nor competent. As the appellate division had noted, the terminally ill woman was mentally incompetent and had no "cognitive ability." The appeals court had ruled that the right to terminate treatment did not encompass incompetent patients but was limited to persons who were irreversibly comatose or brain dead. As Conroy was unable to reason or communicate, there was no way to get her guidance on her own medical care as had been done in other cases involving competent, terminally ill patients.

The appeals court had also drawn a distinction between life-sustaining equipment and artificial feeding. The former was medical treatment, but the latter was the provision of a basic human need that could not rightfully be termed a medical procedure. The court found that withholding nourishment from a patient such as Conroy would actually cause death rather than merely allow a terminal illness to follow its inevitable course. Stopping artificial feeding was tantamount to starving a person to death.

Whittemore's counsel countered that the fact Conroy was incompetent did not empower others to abridge her constitutional right to privacy. She was entitled to basic control over the nature of her medical care. Her nephew, who had known her for over 50 years, had testified on her behalf that she avoided medical treatment and had never visited a doctor prior to becoming incompetent. This was sufficient evidence that she would want the feeding tube removed.

There was no reason, Whittemore's counsel maintained, to distinguish between artificial feeding and other types of life-support measures. Removing a feeding tube was no different on ethical, medical, or legal grounds from disconnecting a respirator or withdrawing other treatment. The feeding tube was an intrusive device. If it had been removed, Conroy would ultimately have died, not from its absence, but from her inability to swallow.

Decision

The New Jersey Supreme Court released its decision in the *Conroy* case on January 17, 1985. The court held that life-sustaining treatment, to include artificial feeding, could be withheld or withdrawn from incompetent, terminally ill patients. The ruling specified that the patient must want the treatment terminated and would "probably die within approximately one year even with the treatment."

The court concluded that "a competent patient has the right to decline any medical treatment . . . and should retain that right when and if he becomes incompetent." Artificial feeding was clearly identified as a form of life-prolonging medical care. "The pain and invasiveness of an artificial feeding device, and the pain of withdrawing that device, should be treated just like the results of administering or withholding any other medical treatment."

Three "best interest tests" were established by the state's highest court for determining the desires of an incompetent patient concerning the cessation of extraordinary life-sustaining measures.

1. The "subjective test": This is the first and most preferred test. "Subjective" refers to the fact the patient has personally and expressly made the decision to halt medical treatment. In the case of an incompetent patient, this decision may have been expressed in a living will, oral directive, or durable power of attorney. It also might be deduced from the patient's previous religious beliefs or reactions to medical care.

2. The "limited-objective test": The second most preferred, this test allows the termination of treatment for patients who have not "unequivocally expressed" their desires prior to becoming incompetent. The treatment would have to prolong suffering and there would have to be some "trustworthy evidence" the patient would want it stopped.

3. The "pure-objective test": Treatment might also be terminated under certain circumstances even when there is no evidence of the patient's desires. It is necessary that the burden of the treatment clearly outweigh any benefits derived and the patient's continuing severe suffering make further administration of the treatment "inhumane."

The court stressed that treatment should never be withdrawn if the patient had expressed the desire to be kept alive regardless of the pain. If there was any doubt, it was best to err "in favor of preserving life." Interestingly, the court noted that Conroy's circumstances would not have satisfied any of the tests.

Impact

Conroy was considered the most far-reaching right-to-die decision yet rendered. The New Jersey Supreme Court had extended the right to terminate life-prolonging care to incompetent patients, had said that artificial feeding was no different from other extraordinary life-sustaining measures, and had held there was no legal distinction between withholding or withdrawing treatment from a dying patient. Although the ruling was not automatically binding in other state courts, *Conroy* had a wide impact across the nation. Many jurisdictions have adopted similar "best interest tests" for use in right-to-die cases.

The *Conroy* decision was controversial. Advocates of the right to die hailed the ruling as a major advancement in the liberty and ability of persons to die with dignity. Opponents saw the decision as one more step down the road to euthanasia. They argued that society was becoming conditioned to the elimination of its burdensome or inconvenient members—which one day would include the elderly, the handicapped, and the retarded.

TUNE V. WALTER REED ARMY MEDICAL HOSPITAL (1985)

Background

The widow of an army officer, Martha Tune was admitted to Walter Reed Army Hospital in February 1985. When she experienced sudden respiratory difficulties, the 71-year-old woman was placed on a respirator. It was determined she had terminal heart cancer as well as a severe, progressive deterioration of her lungs.

Tune was conscious, alert, and aware of her medical condition. She requested the respirator be removed so she could "die with dignity." Her physicians, admitting they would not have ordered the respirator had they known the full extent of her condition, nevertheless would not comply with her request. They contended that army policy prevented the termination of life-support equipment once in place for patients at army medical facilities.

As a military hospital, Walter Reed fell under the jurisdiction of the federal court system. Tune asked the U.S. District Court for the District of Columbia to order the respirator withdrawn.

Legal Issues

Tune argued that the hospital's rule violated her constitutional right to privacy. As a competent adult, she had the right to exercise broad control over her medical case. As a terminally ill patient, she should be allowed to decide for herself whether artificial life-support systems should be removed, even though the action would likely result in her immediate death.

A U.S. attorney represented the military hospital. The government, while maintaining the doctors correctly followed army policy in refusing to disconnect the respirator, took no position on the merits of Tune's request.

Decision

The Federal District Court granted Tune's petition on March 4, 1985. An order was issued directing removal of her life-support system.

Suicide

The decision observed that the U.S. Supreme Court had enunciated a basic privacy right in its landmark rulings in *Griswald v. Connecticut* (1965) and *Roe v. Wade* (1973). Although the highest court had not yet considered right-to-die issues, the latter decision was cited as particularly relevant to individual rights concerning medical treatment. In *Roe v. Wade*, the Supreme Court had stated that a competent adult had a paramount right to control what happened to his or her body. This right, while not absolute, could be limited only to serve a compelling government interest.

The Federal District Court concluded that competent adult patients in federal medical facilities who were terminally ill had a constitutional right to determine whether to allow their lives to be prolonged by artificial means. Two state court decisions, **Satz v. Permutter** and **Bartling v. Superior Court,** were mentioned as evidence of the growing legal consensus concerning a patient's right to refuse treatment. In each case state courts permitted competent adults to direct the removal of life-support equipment.

The decision went on to address the customary four state interests against allowing the termination of life-support measures.

1. Preservation of life: The court recognized society's "transcendent" concern for preserving life, but held that this interest must defer to the right to refuse treatment of a terminally ill adult who was "the best, indeed the only, true judge of how such life as remains to him may best be spent."

2. Prevention of suicide: The question of suicide was not involved in Tune's request because approval was not being sought "to terminate a healthy life by artifical, self-induced means, but merely to allow nature to take its course."

3. Protection of innocent third parties: As in most right-to-die cases, there were no dependents whose interests would be adversely affected by the removal of life-support systems.

4. Integrity of the medical profession: The court stressed that medical ethics incorporated not only the responsibility to "do no harm" but also the obligation to respect the desires of individuals concerning their treatment.

Impact

Tune was the first federal court ruling in a right-to-die case. In its reasoning, the Federal District Court followed the lead of state courts. Most important, the court concurred that the privacy right is the basis for a patient's control over medical decisions to include the cessation of artifi-

86

cial life-support measures. Subsequent lower federal court decisions have reached the same conclusion. In the summer of 1989 the Supreme Court agreed to hear its first right-to-die case. Legal experts point out that the whole area of right-to-die law may well be redefined by the highest court's pending ruling in **Cruzan v. Harmon.**

BOUVIA V. SUPERIOR COURT (1986)

Background

Elizabeth Bouvia was born with cerebral palsy and had been almost completely paralyzed for most of her life. Despite her handicap she earned a bachelor's degree in social work and began graduate studies in fine arts. She had been living on her own for nine years, with considerable assistance from others, when she was voluntarily admitted in 1983 to Riverside General Hospital in her native California.

The 26-year-old woman, who required almost continuous care, realized that she could not realistically hope to lead an independent life in the future and decided she wanted to die. She stopped eating in an effort to starve herself to death. Hospital regulations would not allow a patient to decline all nourishment, however, and she continued to accept liquid proteins.

Bouvia asked the California courts to instruct the hospital to allow her to "discontinue sufficient caloric intake so that she would eventually succumb to starvation." Her request to starve herself captured national attention and thrust the question of a severely impaired person's right to die into public debate. Many argued that she was attempting to commit suicide.

The California trial court hearing the case agreed. In December 1983 the court ruled in *Bouvia v. County of Riverside* that at issue was whether "a severely handicapped, mentally competent person who is otherwise physically healthy and not terminally ill has the right to end her life with the assistance of society." The court found that she did not have the right to kill herself with society's help.

Between 1983 and 1986, Bouvia's medical condition progressively worsened. She was transferred to High Desert Hospital in Los Angeles County. In constant pain from degenerative arthritis, she periodically was administered morphine to relieve her suffering. When the staff at the public hospital determined that she could no longer swallow sufficient nourishment to survive, a nasogastric feeding tube was inserted against her express instructions.

Bouvia sought a court order halting the artificial feeding. The trial court denied her petition and she appealed.

Legal Issues

Bouvia's attorneys maintained that her second application to a court was substantially different from her first. In 1983 she had asked for assistance in starving herself to death. Now she was turning to the courts to protect her constitutional right to refuse medical treatment. It was no longer a question of refusing food she was able to eat, but of directing the removal of an intrusive medical device that had been installed against her will.

Decision

The California Court of Appeal accepted the reasoning of Bouvia's attorneys. In a decision released April 16, 1986, the court ruled that her rejection of artificial feeding was not tantamount to committing suicide. She was, instead, exercising a "basic and fundamental" right to refuse medical treatment.

Bouvia's motives for declining the life-sustaining measure were not relevant. What was important was her right to forgo medical care. The court emphasized that this was "not a conditional right subject to approval by ethics committees or courts-of-law." It involved a "moral and philosophical" decision that could be made by the patient alone.

It had been estimated that Bouvia could survive another 15 to 20 years through artificial feeding. The Court of Appeals found there was no requirement that a patient be "terminally ill" in order to be able to refuse life-sustaining measures. The fact that treatment might significantly prolong an individual's life did not give the medical profession the right to preserve a patient's existence against his or her desires. The decision observed that "It is incongruous, if not montrous, for medical practitioners to assert their right to preserve a life that someone else must live, or, more accurately, endure for 15 to 20 years. We cannot conceive it to be the policy of this State to inflict such an ordeal upon anyone."

Impact

Elizabeth Bouvia remains in a California hospital. Although she won the court order allowing her to direct the removal of her feeding tube, to date she has not done so. She has stated it would be too painful for her to starve herself.

The decision in *Bouvia* represented the first time a court had authorized the cessation of life-support measures for a person who was not terminally ill. The Court of Appeals reiterated a patient's basic right to refuse medical care. Reflecting a growing trend nationwide, the court considered artificial feeding to be no different from other kinds of extraordinary life-sustaining procedures.

The California court did not authorize Bouvia to take her own life. What it did sanction was allowing her to remove the feeding tube that was artificially forestalling her death against her wishes.

BROPHY V. NEW ENGLAND SINAI HOSPITAL (1986)

Background

In March 1983 a blood vessel suddenly burst in the brain of Paul Brophy. The 45-year-old firefighter never regained consciousness. He was diagnosed as being in a persistent vegetative state with no realistic hope of ever recovering. He developed trouble swallowing and doctors inserted a feeding tube into his stomach in December 1983.

A year later Brophy's wife, who had become his guardian, asked New England Sinai Hospital to withdraw the gastrostomy tube. When the hospital refused, Patricia Brophy turned to a Massachusetts probate court for permission to halt the artificial feeding that was keeping her husband alive. The probate court ruled against the removal of the feeding tube and she appealed directly to the Massachusetts Supreme Judicial Court.

Legal Issues

Brophy was unable to indicate for himself his preference concerning life-support measures. His family unanimously agreed he would not want to be maintained in a vegetative state. Patricia Brophy argued that the court should accept a "substituted judgment," where a decision is made for the patient based on what the patient would have chosen in those circumstances, and allow her husband to die with dignity.

The probate court acknowledged it was clear Brophy would not have wanted to receive artificial feeding. The court, however, concluded that the focus should be on the quality of Brophy's care rather than the quality of his life. Otherwise, the court's risked "pronouncing judgment that Brophy's life is not worth preserving." The decision also emphasized that Brophy was not terminally ill. The court observed that only in an instance where a patient would receive no meaningful benefit from the provision of food and water would it be "permissible to remove the feeding tube in accordance with his substituted judgment."

Suicide

Decision

In a 4-to-3 decision, the Supreme Judicial Court ruled on September 11, 1986, that the probate court was wrong not to honor the right of an incompetent patient, through a substituted judgment, to refuse artificial feeding. The state's highest court agreed that Brophy would have wanted to have the feeding tube withdrawn. The majority decision stressed that the constitutional, as well as common, law right to decline medical treatment included the right "to be free of nonconsensual invasion of one's bodily integrity."

Although Brophy was not terminally ill, this did not justify the state overriding his right to discontinue treatment based on an abstract concern for preserving life. In certain circumstances, the majority noted, "the burden of maintaining the corporeal existence degrades the very humanity it was meant to serve. The law recognizes the individual's right to preserve his humanity, even if to preserve his humanity means to allow the natural process of a disease or affliction to bring about death with dignity." If a patient chose to forgo life-saving measures, then it was that individual, and not the state, who was making the decision about the quality of his or her life.

The dissenting judges strongly disagreed with the majority's reasoning. One dissent stated that "the court today has endorsed euthanasia and suicide."

Impact

As evidenced by the dissenting opinions, the *Brophy* decision was controversial. The legal guardian appointed by the court to protect Brophy's interests during the trial claimed that it was apparently "the first step in the selective killing of unproductive citizens." He appealed to the U.S. Supreme Court, which in turn refused to block the order that the feeding tube could be removed.

Brophy was transferred to another facility in Massachusetts where the gastrostomy tube was withdrawn. He died eight days later from pneumonia.

The *Brophy* ruling was the first instance of a state superior court authorizing the termination of artificial feeding in a case where the patient was still alive at the time of the decision. Right-to-die groups hailed the case as an important victory. Massachusetts' highest court had joined a growing number of tribunals across the country that had held that: patients had a right to refuse artificial feeding in the same way as any other extraordinary medical treatment; patients did not have to be terminally ill to exercise this right; and the actual act of declining a life-sustaining measure did not constitute suicide.

IN RE RODAS (1987)

Background

In February 1986 Hector Rodas suffered brain damage from his drug abuse. The 34-year-old man was left paralyzed from the neck down and required constant nursing care. He was unable to swallow and a feeding tube was inserted directly into his stomach. He was also in a permanently "locked-in" state. Although still mentally alert, he could no longer speak. He communicated by moving his head and blinking his eyes.

Rodas indicated that he wanted to halt the artificial feeding that was keeping him alive. The Hilltop Rehabilitation Center where he was a patient would not accede to his request. The center eventually petitioned a Colorado district court for guidance in handling the case. Rodas was represented at the hearing by attorneys associated with the American Civil Liberties Union.

Legal Issues

The court confronted a number of classic right-to-die questions. Was Rodas, as Hilltop maintained, in effect asking the center to assist in his suicide? If not, should the court then force the medical facility to discontinue the treatment it believed necessary to uphold its "mission to rehabilitate the ill"? Or was there a larger purpose to be served in preserving Rodas's life?

Decision

The district court announced its decision on January 22, 1987. Hilltop was ordered to remove the feeding tube. The center was granted immunity from civil or criminal liability that might result from the action.

In its opinion, the court observed that Rodas was not terminally ill in a traditional sense. He was, however, terminally ill in the sense that if he went without medical treatment for several days he would die. His condition was such that he was only being kept alive through modern medical technology. His decision to stop the artificial feeding could not be considered suicide because "suicide . . . does not occur where the natural consequence of a person's illness is death."

Rodas's right to control his medical care took precedence over general state interests in preserving life. This right was rooted in a "clearly established legal and medical ethic that a competent adult is allowed to refuse medical treatment." The court found that Rodas, despite his "locked-in" condition, was sufficiently mentally competent to have given an "informed consent" to halt his artificial nourishment.

The court also concluded that Rodas's basic privacy right prevailed over any position Hilltop might take concerning medical ethics. It did not matter if the center's "conscience" did not permit the withdrawal of life-saving measures. The law prohibited the facility from forcibly feeding a patient against his or her will. "To permit Hilltop to continue this unwanted treatment by Mr. Rodas," the court declared, "would be to permit an ongoing battery to be imposed upon him." The center was required to allow Rodas to terminate his artificial feeding.

Impact

Hilltop did not contest the decision. The feeding tube was removed and Rodas died several weeks later.

Rodas, the first right-to-die decision in Colorado, had national signficiance. Although only a lower court ruling, the opinion stated that a medical institution had to honor a patient's desire to end artificial life-support measures. The court went on to hold that if the institution did not comply, it was potentially liable for a charge of battery against the patient. This position reflected the shifting emphasis in right-to-die cases. Previously facilities had been concerned that allowing a patient to die would expose them to a charge of homicide or aiding a suicide. Increasingly the concern was moving to a facility's liability for not respecting a patient's rights.

The Colorado court was among the first to authorize the cessation of life-sustaining care for a person who was not terminally ill. As the debate in this and subsequent cases would illustrate, the question of whether it was appropriate to consent to the death of a severely impaired person such as Rodas was far from resolved in either the legal system or society in general.

NEW JERSEY CASES (1987)

Background

The New Jersey Supreme Court has been at the forefront of right-to-die legal issues since its landmark ruling in **Quinlan** in 1976. Its decision in **Conroy** in 1985 was considered one of the most far-reaching opinions in a right-to-die case to date. On June 24, 1987, the court released three more significant right-to-die rulings.

The three cases before the court involved patients in different medical conditions and circumstances. In each instance the court had been asked to authorize the withdrawal of artificial life-support systems. Collectively, the court's decisions in the three cases provided a comprehensive set of guidelines on when and how medical treatment might be terminated.

In the first case, *In re Farrell*, a woman in her early 30s had contracted amyotrophic lateral sclerosis (Lou Gehrig's disease). When it was determined that hospitalization could do nothing further for her condition, Kathleen Farrell went home to live with her husband and two sons. She was paralyzed and required a respirator.

In late 1985 Farrell told her husband that she was "tired of suffering" and wanted the respirator disconnected. Francis Farrell sought appointment as his wife's guardian with authority to remove her respirator. The trial court granted his request, but stayed its order until the case could be reviewed at the appellate level. Kathleen Farrell subsequently died while still attached to the respirator, but the New Jersey Supreme Court agreed to hear the case because of its broad relevance.

The second case, *In re Peter*, concerned a woman in her early 60s who remained in a persistent vegetative state following a sudden collapse at home. Hilda Peter had been placed in a nursing home where she was sustained by artificial feeding through a nasogastric tube. Peter previously had signed a power of attorney authorizing her companion, Eberhard Johanning, to make medical decisions on her behalf if she were unable to do so.

In October 1985 a New Jersey superior court named Johanning as Peter's guardian. Following state procedures, he petitioned the Office of Ombudsman for the Institutionalized Elderly for approval to halt the artificial feeding. The Ombudsman, who was charged with safeguarding the welfare of elderly patients in nursing homes, interpreted the New Jersey Supreme Court's decision in **Conroy** to limit the withdrawal of life-sustaining measures to patients who were within one year of death. As the medical prognosis had Peter surviving for "many years, possibly decades," he denied the request. Johanning then appealed directly to the state supreme court.

In re Jobes involved a pregnant 25-year-old woman who was in an automobile accident in 1980. The fetus did not survive and Nancy Ellen Jobes suffered massive, irreversible brain damage. The permanently unconscious woman was eventually moved to the Lincoln Park Nursing Home where she received nourishment through a feeding tube inserted in her abdomen.

In 1985 John Jobes asked the nursing home to stop his wife's artificial

---

feeding. When the nursing home refused, he went to court. After hearings that included a bedside visit, the trial court approved the removal of the feeding tube. Lincoln Park contested the decision to the state's highest court.

Legal Issues

There were a number of common legal threads in the three cases. The most basic question confronting the Supreme Court concerned the right of persons to refuse medical treatment when doing so would result in their deaths. Did this right, which the court already had extended to patients who were close to death, also apply to patients who could be maintained indefinitely in their current condition through modern life-sustaining technology? If the patient was incompetent or unconscious, who should decide whether life-support measures should be withheld or withdrawn? There was also the difficult question of how to ensure a competent patient such as Kathleen Farrell was making an informed decision to end her life.

Two of the cases again raised the troubling issue of whether artificial feeding should be considered a form of medical treatment. Many in the medical profession and elsewhere believed that food and water transcended any definition of health care. The provision of nourishment was basic to human society and could not morally or ethically be withheld, even at the request of a dying patient. In its consideration of artificial feeding, as well as the other questions, the Supreme Court had to weigh the rights of medical personnel and institutions. Was it appropriate to force health care professionals to take actions they felt violated medical ethics?

Decision

The New Jersey Supreme Court decided in favor of the patient's right to die in each case. The court strongly endorsed the principle that patient interests must come before those of the state. In ruling in the three cases, the court stressed its constant goal was "to insure that patients' medical preferences are respected." This included the right to forgo life-sustaining medical care.

Justice Marie L. Garibaldi, who wrote the majority opinion in all three cases, noted that medical choices were ultimately a private matter. They "should not be decided by societal standards of reasonableness or normalcy." It was "the patient's preferences—formed by his or her unique personal experiences—that should control." It did not matter whether a person was able to make medical decisions personally or had to rely on a surrogate. All patients, Garibaldi wrote, "competent or incompetent, with some cognitive ability or in a persistent vegetative state, terminally ill or not terminally ill, are entitled to choose whether or not they want life-sustaining equipment."

The court reaffirmed its ruling in **Conroy** that artificial feeding was a form of medical care. As such, patients were fully within their rights in demanding it be terminated.

In general, medical decisions were best made by the patient together with family and loved ones. In the case of Kathleen Farrell, a competent adult patient, the decision to remove the respirator ultimately belonged to her alone. In instances where patients were no longer able to guide their own medical care, surrogate decision makers should use their knowledge of the patient to arrive at the course of medical treatment the person would have chosen. As Nancy Jobes was in an irreversible vegetative state, her husband was authorized to act in her best interest and direct that artifical feeding be halted.

The court found that the Ombudsman had misinterpreted **Conroy.** Clair Conroy was conscious, although severely impaired, while Hilda Peter was in a persistent vegetative state. There was no requirement to apply a life-expectancy test to a permanently comatose person because there was no meaningful benefit to be gained from continued life in such a condition. Thus Peter's designated surrogate was empowered to order her artificial feeding stopped.

The court underscored the doctor's role in right-to-die decisions. As a safeguard, physicians had to certify a patient was incompetent or unconscious before a surrogate could be appointed. The attending physician could assist patients and their families in reaching difficult decisions. The final determination concerning artificial life-support systems, however, resided outside the medical profession.

The *Jobes* decision attempted to respect the right of medical facilities to set and enforce internal ethical policies. When there was a conflict between patient and medical institution over the cessation of life-support measures, the best answer was the transfer of the patient to another facility. When this was not possible, however, the patient's desires took precedence over the ethical position of either the institution or its medical staff.

Impact

The Lincoln Park Nursing Home sought unsuccessfully to appeal the *Jobes* decision in federal court. During this time Nancy Jobes was moved to another facility. Both she and Hilda Peter died shortly after the removal of their feeding tubes.

The New Jersey Supreme Court had exhaustively examined the right-to-die issue. Its decisions had established a considerable body of case law that would not only guide subsequent medical decision-making in New Jersey but would influence court actions across the nation.

The court observed, though, that it was uncomfortable resolving right-to-die questions. To the extent possible, the justices insisted, such issues belonged more properly in the legislative branch. The court also stressed the importance of documents such as living wills in helping to arrive at treatment decisions for patients who were no longer able to communicate their desires.

CRUZAN V. HARMON (1988)

Background

On the night of January 11, 1983, Nancy Beth Cruzan was thrown from her car in a crash not far from her home in Missouri. It is estimated her brain had been without oxygen for 12 to 14 minutes before paramedics revived her. The 25-year-old woman never regained consciousness. She sank into a persistent vegetative state, incapable of any conscious action, including swallowing. With her parents' consent, a feeding tube was inserted in her stomach.

In early 1987, their hopes for a miraculous recovery having given way to medical reality, Cruzan's parents asked the Missouri Rehabilitation Center to withdraw the feeding tube. The center refused and the Cruzans filed a court action seeking judicial approval of their request. When the trial court sanctioned the termination of Cruzan's artificial feeding, the state attorney general appealed to the Missouri Supreme Court.

Legal Issues

The trial court had accepted the testimony of Cruzan's family that she would not wish to be maintained in the "limbo" of a permanent vegetative state. The court concluded that even though Cruzan no longer had any "cognitive brain functions," her constitutional "right to liberty" still entitled her "to refuse or direct the withholding or withdrawal of artificial death-prolonging procedures." To deny her parents as her coguardians the authority to halt the artificial feeding on her behalf would deprive her of equal protection of the law.

In its appeal, the attorney general's office, representing the state, argued that the only valid consideration in the case was the preservation of life. Missouri had a long statutory tradition of a commitment to life, which would be violated by allowing Cruzan to die. The appeal specifically cited the state's Living Will Act, which expressly forbade the with-holding of food or water from any patient.

Decision

On November 16, 1988, the Supreme Court overturned the lower court's decision. A four-to-three majority ruled that there was "no principled legal basis which permits the co-guardians in this case to choose the death of their ward. In the absence of such a legal basis for that decision and in the face of this state's strongly stated policy in favor of life, we choose to err on the side of life, respecting the right of the incompetent persons who may wish to live despite a severely diminished quality of life."

In its opinion, the majority stated that the case in essence asked the court "to allow the medical profession to make Nancy die by starvation and dehydration." The court refused to sanction Cruzan's death, reasoning that the state's concern for preserving life was an absolute and unqualified interest that took precedence over any rights a patient might have concerning treatment. A number of state statutes, including the preamble to the state's controversial 1986 abortion law, were cited as evidence of Missouri's "strong disposition in favor of preserving life."

The court declined to find an "unfettered right of privacy" in either the federal or state constitutions. There was no solid constitutional basis, the majority concluded, for endorsing the right of a patient to refuse medical care in every circumstance. Although there were circumstances where a terminal patient might forgo life-sustaining measures, outlined in the state's Living Will Act, there was no unequivocal constitutional right that justified allowing patients to do so whenever they so desired. The state's interest in preserving Cruzan's life was "particularly valid," and overrode her alleged wishes, because she was not terminally ill.

The majority also rejected the idea that a patient could make an informed decision in advance about possible medical care. According to the court, it was "definitionally impossible" to anticipate and weigh all the benefits and risks of a hypothetical future medical procedure. In other words, there was no certain way, as Cruzan was unconscious, of determining her desires concerning treatment. Even if the court were to accept the previous declarations of a comatose patient as valid, the evidence of Cruzan's wishes was "woefully inadequate."

Similarly, there was no statutory basis for allowing a guardian to terminate life-sustaining measures on behalf of an incompetent patient. The court attacked the concept of "substituted judgment," where a surrogate attempts to make the decision the patient would have made if able, as "logically inconsistent." If the point was to respect the personal autonomy and privacy of the patient, then it made no sense to permit another person to exercise control over life-and-death decisions.

Finally, the court found that the provision of nourishment was not an aspect of health care. "Common sense tells us that food and water do not treat an illness, they maintain a life." The cessation of artificial feeding for any patient was impermissible.

Impact

The Missouri Supreme Court's decision was a dramatic departure from the growing body of case law on right-to-die issues. The court was the first to rule against the termination of artificial feeding for a permanently comatose patient as well as the first to hold that tube feeding was not medical care. The ruling also went against the legal trend to expand the basic privacy right to incorporate the right of persons to control their medical treatment.

The *Cruzan* decision provoked nationwide debate. Nancy Beth Cruzan became a symbol of the struggle over how best to balance the obligation of society to preserve life and the right of an individual to die with dignity.

The Cruzans appealed to the U.S. Supreme Court. Twenty-three organizations, including the American Medical Association, filed friend-of-the-court briefs urging the nation's highest court to hear the case. In July 1989 the Supreme Court announced it would review the *Cruzan* decision. This marked the first time the tribunal had agreed to address right-to-die issues.

The Supreme Court may use the *Cruzan* case as a vehicle for issuing a broad ruling on the entire right-to-die area. This might include a determination whether the constitutional right to privacy encompasses a right to refuse medical treatment. Legal experts point out, though, that the Court is generally inclined to decide cases on the narrowest possible grounds. In this event, basic right-to-die questions may well continue to be resolved in state court systems.

CHAPTER 4

BIOGRAPHICAL LISTING

Modern ideas about suicide have been shaped by a wide array of individuals. Psychiatrists, theologians, scholars, and scientists, as well as concerned laypeople, have all contributed to the evolving debate over suicide. This chapter contains brief biographical sketches on a cross section of the persons who have figured prominently in the issue of suicide in the United States. Emphasis is on those who have influenced contemporary thinking about suicide. Individuals who committed suicide are included when their actions or the fact of their death had an impact on the larger question of suicide itself.

Each biographical entry provides the years of birth and, when applicable, death; identifies the relationship of the individual to the issue of suicide; and describes the person's significant involvement and impact. Names in bold print indicate individuals who have a separate entry in the listing.

Alfred Alvarez (1929–   )   An English writer and educator, Alvarez is the author of the influential and controversial study of suicide, *The Savage God*. The 1971 book examines mankind's changing attitudes toward suicide from the earliest societies to modern times. Alvarez, who knew **Sylvia Plath**, includes a personal recollection of her final years. The work explores why Plath and many other modern artists decide to commit suicide. Alvarez also recounts his attempt to take his own life.

Jean Baechler (1937–   )   A noted French philosopher, scholar, and educator, Baechler is the author of the highly regarded *Suicides*. In this 1979 book, based on numerous case studies, he characterized suicide as a behavior or strategy for dealing with the existential problems of life. The suicidal motive was identified with a desire for "transfiguration" into a more desirable state. Baechler's controversial conclusions have generated considerable debate among suicidologists.

Christiaan Barnard (1922–   )   A South African surgeon renowned for performing the world's first human heart transplant, Barnard is an outspoken advocate of euthanasia. In 1980 he published *Good Life, Good Death: A Doctor's Case for Euthanasia and Suicide.* Barnard defended active euthanasia as a humane response to suffering and noted that it is already a discretely accepted medical practice.

Elizabeth Bouvia (1957–   )   Almost completely paralyzed by cerebral palsy, Bouvia petitioned a California court in 1983 for the right to starve herself to death. Her request, which was denied, raised the difficult issue of a seriously impaired person's right to die. In 1986 Bouvia, whose condition had worsened, won approval from the courts to halt the artificial feeding that by then was keeping her alive. To date, she has chosen not to terminate the life-sustaining measure.

Paul E. Brophy, Sr. (1937–1986)   A Boston firefighter, Brophy suffered a brain hemorrhage in 1983 and never regained consciousness. In 1986 the Massachusetts courts ruled that his family could terminate the artificial feeding keeping him alive. Brophy's feeding tube was withdrawn in October of the same year and he died shortly thereafter. The case, which drew wide attention, was the first instance of a state's highest court authorizing removal of artificial feeding from a non-terminal patient.

Ruth S. Cavan (1896–   )   Trained as a sociologist at the University of Chicago, Cavan became a leading member of the "Chicago School" of sociology that emerged in the 1920s. These sociologists utilized statistical analyses to examine urban social conditions. Cavan concentrated on the issue of suicide. Her pioneering 1928 study *Suicide* linked higher suicide rates to the social fragmentation of modern urban life.

Nancy Beth Cruzan (1957–   )   Cruzan was in an automobile accident in January 1983. She never regained consciousness and remains in a persistent vegetative state. The Missouri Supreme Court in 1988 ruled that Cruzan's parents could not authorize the termination of the artificial feeding that was keeping her alive. The Supreme Court in 1989 agreed to review the decision, making the *Cruzan* case the first time right-to-die issues would be argued before the highest court. As a consequence, the case has become a focal point of the debate between advocates and opponents of euthanasia.

Alfred B. DelBello (1934–   )   DelBello became active in youth suicide prevention as lieutenant governor of New York. In 1984 he founded the National Committee on Youth Suicide Prevention. DelBello is chairman of the voluntary nationwide organization, which works to reduce youth suicide through research and prevention programs.

Jack D. Douglas (1937–   )   A leading suicidologist, Douglas published in 1967 an influential critique of suicide statistics. In *The Social Meanings of Suicide* he argued that suicide rates were calculated on the basis of imprecise data. As a result, studies of suicide that relied on broad statistics were inherently flawed. A sociologist, Douglas has noted that modern theories on suicide increasingly emphasize a multidisciplinary approach.

Louis I. Dublin (1882–1969)   Dublin was considered the leading authority on health statistics of his time. A brilliant scientist and mathematician who headed the statistics department of a major insurance company, he published *To Be or Not to Be* in 1933. The book presented an exhaustive statistical analysis of suicide. Dublin believed that the actual number of suicides was significantly underreported. The annual award of the American Association of Suicidology is named in his honor.

Emile Durkheim (1858–1917)   A leading French educator and intellectual, Durkheim was a major figure in the development of the modern field of sociology. In 1897 he published *Suicide*, the first systematic sociological study of the subject. Durkheim identified different categories of suicide, each based on the relationship of the individual to society. His now-classic book generated greater interest in suicide and has served as the cornerstone of modern sociological thinking on the issue.

Norman L. Farberow (1918–   )   One of the foremost authorities in the field of suicidology, Farberow was cofounder in 1958, with **Edwin S. Shneidman,** of the famed Los Angeles Suicide Prevention Center. He is currently the center's director as well as a clinical psychology professor at UCLA. Farberow is the author of numerous books, articles, and papers on suicide. He participated in the national Task Force on Youth Suicide, contributing a study on suicide behavior factors.

Joseph F. Fletcher (1905–   )   A theologian and ethicist, Fletcher was a charter member in 1938 of the Euthanasia Society of America (now the Society for the Right to Die). His 1954 book *Morals and Medicine*, which made the case for "voluntary medical euthanasia," brought into public debate the increasingly difficult ethical issues surrounding modern medical care. Fletcher campaigned tirelessly for euthanasia throughout his distinguished career as a clergyman and educator. He is the President Emeritus of the Society for the Right to Die.

Shervert H. Frazier, Jr. (1921–   )   A psychiatrist and educator, Frazier was director of the National Institute of Mental Health when he was appointed chairman of a Task Force on Youth Suicide established in May 1985 by Secretary of Health and Human Services (HHS) Margaret M. Heckler. The task force sponsored three national conferences in 1986 on youth suicide that brought together a wide range of experts in the field. The task force completed its work in October 1987, and Frazier submitted a detailed set of recommendations to then HHS Secretary Otis R. Bowen on the "perplexing problem" of youth suicide.

Sigmund Freud (1856–1939)   The founder of modern psychoanalysis, Freud's ideas have profoundly influenced 20th-century thinking about suicide. In a broad sense, his investigations into the psyche and its control over human behavior are the basis for the now commonly accepted view that suicide is linked to individual psychological problems. Freud specifically addressed the issue of suicide in two famous papers, *Mourning and Melancholia* (1917) and *Beyond the Pleasure Principle* (1920). His theories on depression and the death instinct have shaped subsequent psychoanalytic inquiry into suicide.

Mary E. Giffin (1919–   )   A psychiatrist, Giffin has been a leading researcher into the causes of teenage suicide for many years. Her work has been the subject of articles in many popular magazines and periodicals including *Time*, *McCall's*, and the *Wall Street Journal*. Giffin is the coauthor of *A Cry for Help: Exploring and Exploding the Myths about Teen Suicide—A Guide for All Parents of Adolescents*.

Judith Guest (1936–   )   Guest is the author of the best-selling novel *Ordinary People*. Published in 1976, the novel appeared at a time when the issue of youth suicide was becoming a national concern. The book traces the struggle of a teenage boy and his family to deal with his severe depression and attempted suicide. The work was subsequently made into a highly acclaimed film of the same name that won the 1980 Oscar for best movie of the year. Both the novel and film have been praised for their sensitive treatment of the subject of suicide.

Herbert Hendin (1926–   )   A psychiatrist and educator, Hendin has written a number of influential books on suicide, among them *Black Suicide* (1969), *The Age of Sensation* (1975), and *Suicide in America* (1982). In his work he has attempted to bring together the psychological and sociological theories on suicide. Hendin is an articulate opponent of active euthanasia and efforts to legalize suicide.

Dereck Humphry (1930–   )   A British newspaper reporter for many years, Humphry in 1978 cowrote *Jean's Way*, an account of how he helped his terminally ill first wife commit suicide. British authorities decided not to prosecute Humphry for aiding a suicide, and he subsequently emigrated to the United States. In 1980, together with his second wife, Ann Wickett, he founded the Hemlock Society. The same year the society published a controversial guide on how to commit suicide. As the society's director, as well as an author of several books on euthanasia and a frequent lecturer, Humphry has been at the forefront of the campaign for the right of the hopelessly ill to assisted suicide or "self-deliverance."

James W. (Jim) Jones (1931–1978)   Believing he was a messiah, the Reverend Jim Jones founded the People's Temple of Disciples of Christ in his native Indiana in 1956. He moved his quasi-religious sect to California in 1971. Five years later Jones and roughly 1,000 followers established Jonestown, an agricultural settlement in the jungle of Guyana. On November 18, 1978, Jones and over 900 members of his People's Temple cult took their own lives in a mass suicide.

Francine L. Klagsbrun (–   )   An author and researcher, Klagsbrun wrote the acclaimed best-seller *Too Young to Die: Youth and Suicide*. Her book, first published in 1976, is credited with drawing attention to the subject of youth suicide. She is married to Samuel C. Klagsbrun, a psychiatrist who is active in suicide issues.

Arthur Koestler (1905–1983)   A renowned Hungarian-born author who became a British subject, Koestler was involved in a number of political and social causes. As a vice president for the Voluntary Euthanasia Society in London, he wrote an essay for the organization's booklet "A Guide to Self-Deliverance." On March 3, 1983, Koestler and his wife, Cynthia, were found dead from an overdose of barbiturates. The couple had left a note explaining their suicide pact. Their deaths drew wide attention to the issue of euthanasia.

Emil Kraepelin (1856–1926)   A German professor of psychiatry, Kraepelin is mentioned with **Sigmund Freud** and **Emile Durkheim** as one of the early 20th-century thinkers who shaped the terms of the modern debate over the causes of suicide. Kraepelin maintained that actual physical or organic disorders were behind the psychological problems that led to suicidal behavior. His ideas are evident today in the research into the link between chemical imbalances in the brain and depression.

Elizabeth Kübler-Ross (1926–   )   A psychiatrist and popular author, Kübler-Ross is considered among the leading experts on thanatology. Her books and lectures on death and dying are credited with focusing public interest on these issues.

Robert E. Litman (1921–   )   Currently a director and chief of psychiatry at the Los Angeles Suicide Prevention Center, Litman helped develop the psychological autopsy. He is recognized as one of the foremost experts in the area of suicide and the law. Litman participated in the work of the Task Force on Youth Suicide.

Larry James McAfee (1956–   )   A quadriplegic following a 1985 motorcycle accident, McAfee maintained his life was not worth living. He gained nationwide attention in August 1989 when he filed suit in the Georgia courts for the right to turn off the ventilator that allowed him to breathe so he could die. His case became a symbol of the difficult issues involved in the debate over the nation's treatment of the disabled. Although the courts ruled in his favor, McAfee to date has decided instead to continue his struggle to find a meaningful life.

Ronald W. Maris (1936–   )   A professor of sociology and director of the Center for the Study of Suicide at the University of South Carolina, Maris is a leading figure in American suicidology. He has written numerous studies on the subject of suicide and has served as editor of *Suicide and Life Threatening Behavior*, the official publication of the American Association of Suicidology. His 1981 book, *Pathways to Suicide*, is considered the preeminent example of the current sociological approach to suicide in the United States.

Karl A. Menninger (1893–1990)   A professor of clinical psychiatry who practiced at the famous Menninger Clinic he established with his father, Menninger is considered one of the preeminent figures in American psychiatry. In 1938 he published his major work on suicide, *Man Against Himself*. Menninger found that in each suicidal act there is (1) the wish to kill, (2) the wish to be killed, and (3) the wish to die.

Yukio Mishima (1925–1970)   A noted Japanese writer, Mishima advocated traditional samurai values in opposition to the commercialism and materialism of modern Japan. On November 25, 1970, he and four followers, armed with swords, stormed a national defense headquarters in Tokyo. There, in a dramatic statement of his dedication to restoring an imperial Japan, Mishima committed *seppuku*, the ritual samurai form of suicide.

Marilyn Monroe (1926–1962)   An actress and movie star, Monroe became the sex symbol of her generation. On August 5, 1962, she died from an apparent overdose of sleeping pills. Her death was officially ruled a suicide. In the period following her demise, there was a significant rise in the suicide rate nationwide, as many suicides left notes linking their deaths to hers. Partly because of the still-debated circumstances surrounding her death, Monroe has become a legendary cult figure.

Seymour Perlin (1925–   )   A senior research fellow at the Kennedy Institute's Center for Bioethics as well as a professor of psychiatry at George Washington University, Perlin is recognized as one of the nation's foremost experts on suicide. He is the chairman of the Youth Suicide National Center, which he founded in 1985, and took an active part in the federal Task Force on Youth Suicide. He is the editor of the definitive collection *A Handbook for the Study of Suicide.*

Sylvia Plath (1932–1963)   A novelist and poet, Plath addressed themes of emotional and psychological conflict, death, and suicide in her works. On February 11, 1963, she killed herself by breathing the gas from her kitchen stove. Plath has become the symbol of the relationship of the modern poet, and the modern woman, to suicide. In 1971 **Alfred Alvarez** wrote a controversial book, *The Savage God,* which addressed Plath's last days and death.

Charles Francis Potter (1885–1962)   A Baptist minister who assisted the defense as a Bible expert in the famous Scopes trial, the Reverend Potter was an ardent advocate of voluntary euthanasia. In 1938 he founded the Euthanasia Society of America (now the Society for the Right to Die). Potter served as the society's first president and remained active in the euthanasia debate throughout his life.

Karen Ann Quinlan (1954–1985)   Quinlan suffered respiratory failure in April 1975 and fell into a coma. In March 1976 the New Jersey Supreme Court ruled that her family could terminate the medical procedures that were keeping her alive in a persistent vegetative state. The Quinlan case sparked widespread debate over euthanasia and the right to die. The case set a major precedent for other court decisions supporting a terminal patient's right to discontinue life support measures. Removed from her respirator, Quinlan remained in a coma until her death in 1985.

Betty Rollin (1936–   )   A television news correspondent, Rollin revealed in *Last Wish* (1985) that she helped her terminally ill mother commit suicide in 1983. The book recounted how her mother, in constant suffering, had expressed her "last wish" to end her own life. In interviews after the work's publication, Rollin maintained that obtaining the lethal drug overdose for her mother, because it was indirect rather than direct assistance, did not constitute a violation of the New York State law against promoting suicide. The book sparked wide debate over the ethics of aiding a suicide and the related issue of euthanasia.

Jo Roman (1917–1979)   An artist and former social worker, Roman was an outspoken advocate of active euthanasia, or "self-termination." In 1978 she was diagnosed as having breast cancer. After a "debilitating" experience with chemotherapy, she decided to commit suicide, calling it a "rational and artistic option." On June 10, 1979, after careful preparations, she gathered close intimates in her Manhattan apartment to help her complete a "life sculpture" in a coffinlike pine box, drank a farewell champagne toast, and then took her own life with a fatal dose of Seconal. The following year a controversial documentary filmed in the weeks before her death, "Choosing Suicide," was broadcast on public television. Roman meant her well-publicized suicide—she also left a note and a manuscript—to serve as a statement for euthanasia. At the least, it provoked substantial debate on the issue.

Charlotte P. Ross (1932–   )   The founding director in 1966 of the suicide prevention center in San Mateo County, California, Ross was appointed president and executive director of the Youth Suicide National Center in 1985. She played a key role in the enactment in California of the first legislation in the country mandating a statewide program on youth suicide prevention in public schools. Ross is the author of numerous publications on suicide and is a frequent lecturer and consultant in the field.

Edwin S. Shneidman (1918–   )   Currently professor of thanatology at UCLA, Shneidman has been at the forefront of the field of suicidology since the early 1950s. He was a cofounder in 1958, with **Norman L. Farberow,** of the pioneering Los Angeles Suicide Prevention Center. Shneidman subsequently served as the charter director of the Center for the Study of Suicide Prevention at the National Institute of Mental Health. In 1968 he founded the American Association of Suicidology. Shneidman has written extensively on the subject of suicide. More recently he was a member of the federal Task Force on Youth Suicide.

Erwin Stengel (1902–1973)   Born in Vienna where he studied with **Sigmund Freud,** Stengel emigrated to England in 1938. A professor of psychiatry at several universities, he was ranked among the world's preeminent authorities on suicide. His 1964 book *Suicide and Attempted Suicide* is considered one of the classic studies of the subject.

Thomas Szasz (1920–   )   A psychiatrist and author, Szasz has been an outspoken and controversial advocate of the right to suicide. He has argued, in books such as *Law, Liberty, and Psychiatry,* that modern psychiatry labels suicidal persons as mentally ill as a justification for exercising control over their behavior. Szasz maintains an individual has a basic right to commit suicide and efforts at intervention or treatment are actually an infringement on personal liberty.

(Edward) Chad Varah (1911–   )   While rector of a parish in London, the Reverend Dr. Varah founded the Samaritans in 1953. Established as an unofficial Christian lay order dedicated to befriending the suicidal and despairing, the organization has evolved into an international network of branches recognized for their work in suicide prevention. Varah has been widely honored for his lifelong commitment to the Samaritans and its mission.

Gregory Zilboorg (1890–1959)   A Russian-born psychiatrist who emigrated to the United States with his parents at an early age, Zilboorg played a major role in the debate emerging in the early 1930s over the causes of suicide. He argued that the sociological approach to suicide, with its emphasis on statistics, was suspect at best because it relied on incomplete and inaccurate numbers. Most important, it failed to take into account the individual psychology of the suicide victim. For Zilboorg, suicide was ultimately the result of personal trauma rather than sociological conditions.

PART II

GUIDE TO FURTHER RESEARCH

CHAPTER 5

INFORMATION ON SUICIDE

Suicide is a focus of wide professional interest. Numerous books, articles, studies, and papers address every aspect of the phenomenon. Recent attentioin to the question of youth suicide has caused an even greater output of materials on the topic. Resources now include audiovisual (AV) items and computer databases. This chapter is a brief primer on research into self-destructive behavior. After describing the principal reference tools used in finding information on suicide, it then profiles some of the primary works on the subject.

A standard, medium-size municipal or school library will contain much of the information on suicide normally sought by students and others interested in the topic. Several basic library reference resources facilitate identifying and locating materials on self-destructive behavior.

CARD CATALOGS

The card catalog remains a key reference tool. It is a central inventory of a library's holdings, from books and periodicals, to AV materials and microfilms. The catalog contains individual bibliographic citations on all items in the library. Some larger facilities maintain separate catalogs for AV materials, noncirculating reference works, government documents, and special collections.

While most libraries utilize the traditional manual card catalog, a growing number are converting to automated systems. The advent of automated catalogs has marked a parallel trend toward interlibrary networks. Computers allow libraries to cross-reference holdings more readily. With this capability, public and school facilities are joining in cooperative lending systems. A library that is part of such a network now has access to vastly enlarged resources.

AUTOMATED SYSTEMS

Automated, or computer-based, information systems and services have emerged as major research tools. Online and CD ROM systems offer quick access to numerous databases encompassing a broad range of subjects. "Online" means that the library subscribes to a regional, national, or international database network, accessed over a phone line. "CD ROM" is a system of information storage on laser disks for use with microcomputers.

Most of these databases furnish bibliographic citations and abstracts of articles, documents, books, and reports. Some provide the full text of articles. Computer-based systems are particularly helpful because they are updated frequently and therefore capture the most current resources and information.

Several automated databases and information systems are valuable guides to the extensive book and periodical literature on suicide. *InfoTrac*, which indexes mainstream and generally accessible periodical sources, is easy to use and widely available. It provides bibliographic records from more than 900 business, technical, and general interest magazines and newspapers. *InfoTrac* covers the current year plus the three preceding years. *WILSONLINE* provides the full range of printed H. W. Wilson Co. indexes. Users have access to *Book Review Digest, General Science Index, Humanities Index, Reader's Guide to Periodical Literature,* and *Social Science Index.* These and the other indexes available on *WILSONLINE* identify some of the most recent suicide sources.

MEDLINE, an online service of the National Library of Medicine, provides post-1980 bibliographic citations to technically oriented articles on suicide research and health policy issues. The *Health Information Network* (HIN) is a full-text database network that provides health care professionals access to up-to-date suicide information from journalism, agencies of the federal government, and the courts.

INDEXES

Indexes are an integral part of a library's reference complement. These guides compile citations on books, magazine literature, newspaper articles, scholarly tracts, government publications, filmstrips, audio recordings, and historical materials. The book- or pamphlet-form indexes and the automated information systems overlap significantly. Some guides appear both in the traditional printed form and in automated forms. Other indexes are converting from print to computer-based systems.

Book Review Index is a guide to book reviews published in over 300 magazines and newspapers. This bimonthly publication furnishes just citations to the reviews. The monthly *Book Review Digest* provides citations to reviews of current English-language fiction and nonfiction. In addition, the *Digest* prints excerpts from the reviews, which are drawn from some 90 selected periodicals and journals. Sheehy's *Guide to Reference Books* is a good source for annotated citations to reference books.

Major city daily newspapers can be excellent sources on many aspects of suicide. *The New York Times* gives full coverage to major legal, political, social, and cultural developments. *The New York Times Index* is an invaluable research tool for anyone interested in contemporary suicide issues. It concisely summarizes all articles and gives citations to the dates, pages, and columns on which they appeared. Back issues of *The New York Times* and some other major dailies are recorded on microfilm. The *Newspaper Index* is a monthly publication that indexes major newspapers, such as the *Chicago Tribune, Los Angeles Times, Denver Post, Detroit News,* and *San Francisco Chronicle.*

The periodical literature on suicide is substantial. Two sources stand out as sources for articles in mainstream publications. The *Reader's Guide to Periodical Literature* indexes more than 200 general-interest periodicals published in the United States; *Magazine Index* compiles citations to the approximately 370 popular magazines and professional journals. Other indexes track the periodical literature on subject areas in the social sciences and liberal arts. *Social Science Index, Humanities Index,* and *Education Index* cite articles from publications devoted to these disciplines.

The *Encyclopedia of Associations* is standard to any basic library reference collection. A guide to national and international organizations, it provides short explanatory abstracts on each entry. The *Encyclopedia of Associations: Regional, State and Local Organizations* is a seven-volume, geographically organized guide to more than 50,000 nonprofit organizations on the state, city, or local level. Both of these indexes are available online.

GOVERNMENT DOCUMENTS

The federal and state governments issue a variety of information on suicide. These materials are made available to the public through the depository library system. A depository member library—it could be a college facility or a municipal library—receives government publications and maintains a government documents collection. The *Monthly Catalog*

---

of United States Government Publications has bibliographic entries for virtually all documents published by federal agencies, including books, reports, studies, and serials. The *Monthly Catalog* also is available on CD ROM, where it is called *GPO Silverplatter.*

The *Index to U.S. Government Periodicals* covers periodicals of the federal government. *Congressional Information Service Index* (CIS), a directory to the publications of the U.S. Congress, is an excellent source. It is the primary tool for locating documents issued by the various committees of both houses of Congress: hearings, committee prints, reports, and public laws. This source is issued in two parts. One volume is the index. The other volume contains abstracts on the cited publications.

The methods for cataloging public documents vary. Generally, libraries maintain a separate catalog for federal and state government sources. Certain government documents may also be housed in the reference or general book collections, in which event they most likely are listed in the main card catalog.

Probably the finest easily accessible source on the federal government's activities is the *Congressional Quarterly Almanac.* Published annually, it provides a comprehensive overview of political developments, legislative initiatives, and activities of Congress, the White House, and the Supreme Court. For brief summaries of Senate and House bills and information on the status of legislation before Congress, readers should check Commerce Clearing House's *Congressional Index.*

LEGAL RESEARCH

In recent years right-to-die questions have become a matter of increasing litigation. Facility with a few basic legal research tools will benefit anyone who is interested in following legal developments. Morris L. Cohen's *How to Find the Law* is a helpful guide for newcomers to legal research. It discusses basic techniques and describes the main references encountered in researching court decisions and legislative history. *The Guide to American Law: Everyone's Legal Encyclopedia*, a comprehensive source written for the layperson, covers all aspects of the American legal system and includes helpful articles on landmark court cases.

The New York Times provides coverage of major state and federal court rulings. Normally, the *Times* includes background information and analysis, along with excerpts from the majority decision. The *Index to Legal Periodicals* can also prove helpful. It includes a subject and author index, a separate table of cases, and a book review index.

Computerized research can accelerate dramatically the process of locating legal resources. But these online services are expensive, and legal nonprofessionals invariably have problems gaining access to them. The two leading services are *LEXIS* (Meade Data) and *WESTLAW* (West Publishing Company). Both are full-text databases containing federal and state case law, statutes, and administrative regulations.

BASIC SOURCES

Chapter 6 provides an annotated bibliography of a broad cross-section of materials and resources on suicide. Following is a discussion of some basic sources that cover the major aspects and issues involved.

Several books offer a good introduction to the topic. *Suicide in America*, by Herbert Hendin, provides an accessible and broad overview. The highly regarded *Handbook for the Study of Suicide*, edited by Seymour Perlin, is an anthology of pieces by leading experts on the various theories and issues associated with self-destructive behavior. *Definition of Suicide*, by Edwin S. Shneidman, is an explanation of the phenomenon by one of today's preeminent suicidologists. An international perspective on suicide can be obtained from *Suicide in Different Cultures*, by another prominent authority, Norman L. Farberow.

Readers interested in youth suicide can turn to two highly readable works, both intended for the layperson: *A Cry for Help: Exploring and Exploding the Myths about Teenage Suicide—A Guide for All Parents of Adolescents*, by Mary Giffin and Carol Felsenthal, and *Too Young To Die: Youth and Suicide*, by Francine Klagsbrun. The novel *Ordinary People*, by Judith Guest, portrays the human dimension of the troubling problem. A comprehensive analysis of youth suicide is included in the findings of the federal task force on youth suicide. The four-volume *Report of the Secretary's Task Force on Youth Suicide* represents the most current professional thinking on the subject. The incidence of multiple suicides, often linked to the young, is addressed in *Suicide Clusters*, by Loren Coleman.

For the serious student, there are several classic texts worth noting. First published in 1897, Emile Durkheim's *Suicide* is considered the single most influential work on the subject. Two works by Sigmund Freud, "Mourning and Melancholia" in *Collected Papers*, vol. 4, and *Beyond the Pleasure Principle*, laid the foundation for psychoanalytic inquiry into self-destructive behavior. The renowned psychiatrist Karl Menninger expounded upon Freud's theories in his major study *Man Against Himself*.

Contemporary thinking on suicide increasingly reflects a multidisciplinary approach. *Self-Destruction in the Promised Land*, by Howard I. Kushner, provides a thorough review of current research on possible neurobiological factors in self-destructive behavior and suggests an explanation of suicide that integrates culture, psychology, and biology. *Suicide*, by the noted French scholar Jean Baechler, has generated much discussion. Baechler draws on a number of disciplines in his examination of the motivations behind suicide.

Two of the most highly regarded theoretical works in recent years are *The Social Meanings of Suicide*, by Jack D. Douglas, and *Pathways to Suicide*, by Ronald Maris. Each combines a basic sociological methodology with other approaches and insights.

A very useful general resource is the *Encyclopedia of Suicide*, edited by Glen Evans and Norman L. Farberow. An introductory essay covers the history of both the practice and study of suicide. A similar historical treatment, with a literary emphasis, is found in *The Savage God: A Study of Suicide*, by the English poet and critic Alfred Alvarez. Centered on a memoir of the American poet Sylvia Plath, who killed herself in 1963, *The Savage God* is an interesting exploration of the artist's relationship to suicide.

Suicide has been a matter of philosophical debate throughout recorded history. *Suicide: The Philosophical Issues*, edited by M. P. Battin and D. P. Mayo, and *Ethical Issues in Suicide*, edited by M. P. Battin, review the different issues and approaches. A famous modern inquiry into suicide is Albert Camus's "The Myth of Sisyphus," in his *The Myth of Sisyphus and Other Essays*.

The question of a person's right to die is examined in James Rachel's *The End of Life: Euthanasia and Mortality*. The case for euthanasia is made by the famous heart surgeon Dr. Christiaan Barnard in *Good Life, Good Death*. The psychiatrist Thomas Szasz goes one step further in *Law, Liberty and Psychiatry: An Inquiry into the Social Uses of Mental Health Practices*, arguing that individuals have a right to take their own lives. The opposite position is effectively represented in William V. Rauscher's *The Case Against Suicide*.

Several controversial books have recounted the author's involvement in helping a terminally ill loved one to die. Betty Rollin, in *Last Wish*, tells how she assisted her mother to end her life. *Jean's Way*, by Derek Humphry and Ann Wickett, reveals Humphry's role in his first wife's self-inflicted death. Humphry, a cofounder of the pro-euthanasia Hemlock Society, outlines his support for "self-deliverance" in *Right to Die: Understanding Euthanasia*, with Ann Wickett.

Chapter 7 identifies state and local organizations that are a source of information and materials on suicide. National organizations involved in the issue are also listed there. Several warrant specific mention.

The American Association of Suicidology (AAS) is the professional organization of those involved in suicide studies and prevention activities. The AAS serves as a national clearinghouse for information on self-destructive behavior. The association also produces pamphlets and other resources for the general public. Its quarterly journal, *Suicide and Life-Threatening Behavior*, is a leading source for current developments in the field.

Specific materials on adolescent suicide can be obtained from the Youth Suicide National Center. The private, nonprofit organization also operates an information clearinghouse.

The principal organization active in the debate over right-to-die issues is the Society of the Right to Die. The society makes available brochures, pamphlets, and other materials on current medical, legislative, and legal developments. It maintains a range of resources on the living will and publishes an excellent set of booklets on right-to-die court cases.

The Bureau of Health Statistics, part of the Public Health Service, is responsible for assembling and preparing national suicide statistics. These numbers are published in *Monthly Vital Statistics Report*. An annual synopsis is provided in *Vital Statistics of the United States, Volume II, Mortality*.

CHAPTER 6

ANNOTATED BIBLIOGRAPHY

This chapter is an annotated listing of suicide sources. It includes materials drawn from a broad range of print and other media. Separate listings are provided for bibliographies, books, encyclopedias, periodicals, articles, government documents, brochures and pamphlets, and audiovisual materials. Each item is identified by a standard library citation. A brief annotation then describes the resource's contents and scope.

Quite a bit of material is available on self-destructive behavior. Two basic rules have guided the inclusion of materials in this bibliography. First, emphasis is on sources that are available in a medium-size public or school library. Second, items have been selected for their usefulness to students and others doing general research on suicide. Highly technical works on the subject have not been included. Readers desiring further specialized information should consult either the listing of bibliographies in this chapter or the discussion of reference sources in Chapter 5.

BIBLIOGRAPHIES

Allen, N. H. "An Annotated Bibliography to Suicide and Life-Threatening Behavior." *Suicide and Life-Threatening Behavior* 15 (Fall 1985), entire issue.

An annotated bibliography to the periodical, covering volumes 1 to 13, 1971 to 1983.

Farberow, Norman L. *Bibliography on Suicide and Suicide Prevention, 1897–1970*. Washington, D.C.: U.S. Government Printing Office, 1972.

A comprehensive listing of resources by a leading expert on the subject.

Lester, David, B. H. Sell, and K. D. Sell. *Suicide: A Guide to Information Sources*. Detroit: Gale Research Co., 1980.

A broad listing of resources on the subject.

McIntosh, John L. *Suicide Among U.S. Racial Minorities: A Comprehensive Bibliography*. Monticello, Ill.: Vance Bibliographies, 1981.

Provides resources on self-destructive behavior among minority racial groups.

————*Research on Suicide: A Bibliography*. Westport, Conn.: Greenwood Press, 1985.

Includes more than 2,300 citations from books, journals, government documents, proceedings, and dissertations. Also identifies specific journals, computer databases, and associations related to suicide.

Traufman, J., and C. Pollard. *Literature and Medicine: An Annotated Bibliography*. Pittsburgh: University of Pittsburgh Press, 1982.

In a section on suicide, lists novels, poems, and dramas on the subject.

BOOKS

GENERAL

Alvarez, Alfred. *The Savage God: A Study of Suicide*. New York: Random House, 1972.

Explores various theories of suicide, the history of the practice, and changing attitudes throughout the centuries. Also discusses the lives of many 20th-century artists who chose to commit suicide. Alvarez, a noted English poet and critic, reveals that he made an attempt on his own life.

Anderson, Olive. *Suicide in Victorian and Edwardian England*. New York: Oxford University Press, 1987.

Study of suicide in late 19th- and early 20th-century England.

Baechler, Jean. *Suicides.* New York: Basic Books, 1979.

Theoretical work by a noted French scholar that divides suicide into two categories, personal and institutional. Each category is divided into the same ten types—flight, grief, punishment, vengeance, crime, blackmail, appeal, sacrifice, ordeal, and game.

Battin, M. P. *Ethical Issues in Suicides.* Englewood Cliffs, N.J.: Prentice-Hall, 1982.

Examines the various ethical questions raised by suicide.

Battin, M. P., and D. J. Mayo, eds. *Suicide: The Philosophical Issues.* New York: St. Martin's Press, 1980.

Writings on the different philosophical approaches to and understandings of suicide.

Becker, Ernest. *The Denial of Death.* New York: The Free Press, 1973.

Pulitzer Prize–winning study that advances the theme that the fear of death is a universal dimension of human experience.

Bettelheim, Bruno. *The Uses of Enchantment: The Meaning and Importance of Fairy Tales.* New York: Alfred A. Knopf, 1976.

Bettelheim identifies the importance that fairy tales and myths have in children's lives and notes that a common theme is the fear of being separated from one's parents. He suggests that the suicidal adolescent is likely to be someone who either never experienced a trusting family relationship or was separated from this relationship.

Bozarth-Campbell, Alla. *Life Is Goodbye, Life Is Hello: Grieving Well Through All Kinds of Loss.* Minneapolis, MN: CompCare, 1982.

The author describes grief, discusses problem situations, and suggests ways to help along the grieving process.

Burton, Robert. *The Anatomy of Melancholy.* New York: AMS Press, 1983.

First published in 1621, the book is an early study of melancholy and its relationship to suicide.

Camus, Albert. *The Myth of Sisyphus and Other Essays.* New York: Alfred A. Knopf, 1975.

In the "Myth of Sisyphus," the Nobel Prize–winning author examines the philosophical problem of suicide.

Cavan, Ruth Shonle. *Suicide.* Chicago: University of Chicago Press, 1928.

Classical sociological investigation of suicide in urban areas.

Annotated Bibliography

Cheyne, George. *The English Malady*. Delmar, N.Y.: Scholars Facsimiles and Reprints, 1976.

A famous study, first published in 1733, that related suicide in England to environmental conditions.

Choron, Jacques. *Suicide*. New York: Scribner's, 1972.

Approaches suicide from a philosophical and historical viewpoint. Includes an introduction to the topic and discussion of several suicide theories.

Coleman, Loren. *Suicide Clusters*. Boston: Faber and Faber, 1987.

Describes suicide clusters in a historical context, from the waves of suicides by the early Christian church followers to a series of eight elderly murder-suicides in Florida in 1987. Also addresses the dramatic rise of the youth suicide cluster phenomenon in the 1980s.

Colgrove, Melba, Harold H. Bloomfield, and Peter McWilliams. *How to Survive the Loss of a Love*. New York: Bantam, 1976.

Presents 58 activities to do to survive the pain of loss, work through the grief, and begin to heal.

Cornwell, John. *Earth to Earth*. New York: Ecco Press, 1984.

An examination of the probable murder/suicide of three elderly members of a distinguished farming family in Devon, England. The author relates the family history drawn from letters, photographs, diaries, postcards, and legal documents.

Cutter, F. *Art and the Wish to Die*. Chicago: Nelson-Hall, 1983.

Addresses the relationship among art, literature, and the subject of suicide. Includes lists of artists who took their own lives.

DeSpelder, Lynne A., and Albert Strickland. *The Last Dance: Encountering Death and Dying*. Palo Alto, Calif.: Mayfield, 1983.

Discusses the theoretical, practical, and personal aspects of death and explores various perspectives and attitudes on death and dying.

Donne, John. *Biathanatos*. New York: Arno, 1977.

Written in 1608 and published posthumously in 1644, this was the first defense of suicide to appear in English.

Douglas, Jack D. *The Social Meanings of Suicide*. Princeton: Princeton University Press, 1967.

Study by a leading suicidologist that points out the unreliability of official statistics on suicide. Douglas attempts to synthesize broad social factors with personal motivations in explaining the causes of self-destructive behavior.

Dublin, Louis I. *The Facts of Life from Birth to Death*. New York: Macmillan, 1951.

Presents a statistical portrait of suicide.

————*Suicide: A Sociological and Statistical Study*. New York: Ronald Press, 1963.

A sociological study of suicide based on a detailed statistical analysis by one of this century's principal demographers of suicide.

Dublin, Louis I., and B. Bunzel. *To Be or Not to Be: A Study of Suicide*. New York: Smith and Haas, 1933.

An early example of the use of sophisticated statistical methodologies. Considered a classic text.

Durkheim, Emile. *Suicide*. Glencoe, Ill.: The Free Press, 1951.

A comprehensive theory of suicide by the noted French sociologist, originally published in 1897. The first such study based on the new discipline of sociology, the work has profoundly influenced subsequent inquiry into the subject.

Evans, Glen, and Norman L. Farberow. *The Encyclopedia of Suicide*. New York: Facts On File, 1988.

Contains over 500 entries exploring the sociological, psychological, historical, and religious aspects of suicide. Appendixes cover statistics and sources of information. An introductory essay by Dr. Farberow reviews the historical practice and study of suicide.

Farberow, Norman L. *Suicide in Different Cultures*. Baltimore: University Park Press, 1975.

Analyzes the meaning and place of suicide in various cultures.

————*The Many Faces of Suicide: Indirect Self-Destructive Behavior*. New York: McGraw-Hill, 1980.

Discusses the various types of indirect self-destructive behavior.

Farberow, Norman L., and Edwin S. Shneidman, eds. *The Cry for Help*. New York: McGraw-Hill, 1961.

Identifies the attempt at suicide with a "cry for help."

Freud, Sigmund. "Mourning and Melancholia," in *Collected Papers*, vol. 4. London: Hogarth Press, 1949.

Famous essay in which Freud identifies suicide with depression (melancholy) and the turning of aggression back upon oneself (mourning). First published in 1917, the paper strongly influenced psychoanalytic thinking on suicide.

———*Beyond the Pleasure Principle*. London: Hogarth Press, 1950.

Classic text by the founder of psychoanalysis in which he postulates the existence of a death instinct. This instinct is a factor in self-destructive behavior. The work was first published in 1922.

Friedman, Myra. *Buried Alive: The Biography of Janis Joplin*. New York: William Morrow, 1973.

Biography of the pop singer Janis Joplin, who died of an overdose of heroin in 1970.

Gernsbacher, Larry Morton. *The Suicide Syndrome: Origins, Manifestations, and Alleviation of Human Self-Destructiveness*. New York: Human Sciences Press, 1985.

An analysis of suicidal motivations and measures to control their expression.

Gordon, Sol. *When Living Hurts*. New York: Dell, 1988.

A guide to help those contemplating suicide to recognize and cope with the feelings that may lead to self-destruction.

Grollman, Earl A. *Suicide: Prevention, Intervention, Postvention*. Boston: Beacon Press, 1971.

Discusses suicide prevention and treatment measures.

Headley, Lee A. *Suicide in Asia and the Near East*. Berkeley: University of California Press, 1983.

Overview of self-destructive behavior in the region.

Hendin, Herbert. *Suicide and Scandinavia*. New York: Grune and Stratton, 1964.

Investigates the incidence of self-destructive behavior in the region.

———*Black Suicide*. New York: Basic Books, 1969.

The results of a study into suicide among Afro-Americans, particularly in urban areas.

————*The Age of Sensation*. New York: W. W. Norton, 1975.

Presents the results of psychoanalytic investigation into the life-styles and problems of young adults, based on studies of college students at Columbia University during the 1970s. Explores the use of drugs and the emphasis on sensation among the young.

————*Suicide in America*. New York: W. W. Norton, 1982.

Highly regarded overview on all aspects of the subject.

Henry, Andrew, and James Short. *Suicide and Homicide: Some Economic, Sociological and Psychological Aspects of Aggression*. Salem, N.H.: Ayer Company Publishers, Inc., 1977.

Concludes from a study of suicide and economic prosperity that certain groups are more apt to commit suicide because of fluctuations in economic status. Reprint of 1954 ed.

Hewitt, John H. *After Suicide*. Philadelphia: Westminster Press, 1980.

Hewett, a Christian minister, describes ten "games" that families play with each other in the aftermath of a suicide and recommends instead that they keep the lines of communication open.

Holinger, Paul C. *Violent Deaths in the United States: An Epidemiologic Study of Suicide, Homicide, and Accidents*. New York: Guilford Press, 1987.

This work is divided into three parts: epidemiological patterns (1900–1980); relationships between the three types of violent death; and the prediction of violent death rates. Two appendixes provide tables of annual suicide, homicide, and accident mortality rates by factors such as age, gender, and race.

Howland, Bette. *W-3*. New York: Viking Press, 1974.

Account of a women's experience living in a psychiatric ward after attempting suicide.

Hume, David. *An Essay on Suicide*. Yellow Springs, Ohio: Kahoe and Co., 1929.

Famous short essay by the philosopher in which he argued that suicide is not a crime. First published in 1783.

Iga, Mamoru. *The Thorn in the Chrysanthemum: Suicide and Economic Success in Modern Japan*. Berkeley: University of California Press, 1986.

A study of suicide in postwar Japan, the book also describes the lives of five Japanese writers who took their own lives.

Annotated Bibliography

Kraepelin, Emil. *Lectures on Clinical Psychiatry*. New York: Hafner, 1968.

Reprint of the 1904 edition of the German psychiatrist's lectures on the connection between suicidal behavior and mental disturbances. Kraepelin viewed suicide as having an organic basis, anticipating the findings of modern neurobiology.

Kreitman, Norman. *Parasuicide*. London: Wiley, 1977.

The author coins the term "parasuicide" to describe a nonfatal act where an individual deliberately causes self-injury. Parasuicide is different from attempted suicide in that it does not imply suicidal intent.

Kübler-Ross, Elizabeth. *On Death and Dying*. New York: Macmillan, 1970.

An influential best-seller that examines the various stages one may experience when facing death. Kübler-Ross also addresses the subject of suicide, identifying different categories of seriously ill patients who contemplate killing themselves.

Kushner, Howard I. *Self-Destruction in the Promised Land: A Psychocultural History*. New Brunswick, N.J.: Rutgers University Press, 1989.

An interdisciplinary history of suicide in the United States. The author examines the various theories on the causes of suicide and then offers an explanation that integrates culture, psychology, and biology.

Langone, John. *Death Is a Noun: A View of the End of Life*. Boston: Little, Brown, 1972.

Recommends education on death and dying, including suicide.

Lester, David. *Why People Kill Themselves*. Springfield, Ill.: Charles C. Thomas, 1982.

An examination of the causes of suicide.

Linzer, Norman, ed. *Suicide: The Will to Live vs. the Will to Die*. New York: Human Sciences Press, 1984.

Collection of writings on the self-destructive impulse.

Lopez, Alan D., comp. *Suicide and Self-Inflicted Injury*. Geneva: World Health Organization, 1986.

Papers on suicide providing an international perspective.

Lukas, Christopher, and Henry M. Seiden. *Silent Grief: Living in the Wake of Suicide*. New York: Scribner's 1987.

Describes the emotional responses that occur when a loved one commits suicide, such as bereavement, guilt, and hidden or displaced anger. Includes an appendix on self-help and mutual-support groups.

Maris, Ronald. *Pathways to Suicide*. Baltimore: The Johns Hopkins University Press, 1981.

Major theoretical work based on case studies by a leading suicidologist.

———*Biology of Suicide*. New York: Guilford Press, 1986.

Multidisciplinary study reflecting recent advances in research.

Mead, George Herbert. *Mind, Self and Society*. Chicago: University of Chicago Press, 1934.

Influential work on the relationship of the individual to society.

Meerlo, Joost A. M. *Suicide and Mass Suicide*. Chicago: Grune and Stratton, 1962.

Investigates the nature of suicide.

Menninger, Karl A. *Man Against Himself*. New York: Harcourt, Brace and Co., 1938.

Now-classic work by the noted psychiatrist and proponent of Freud's theory that suicide is aggression turned upon the self.

Montaigne, Michel E. *Essais*, edited by A. Thibaudet. Paris: Gallinard, 1958.

Montaigne first writes in support of suicide, but later reverses his stand and concludes that the only acceptable reasons for killing oneself are extreme pain or a worse death.

Morselli, Henry. *Suicide, an Essay on Comparative Moral Statistics*. New York: Ayer, 1975.

Reprint of a late 19th-century study of suicide statistics and their relation to "cosmico-natural" aspects such as climate, biological factors, social conditions, and psychological influences.

Perlin, Seymour, ed. *A Handbook for the Study of Suicide*. New York: Oxford University Press, 1975.

An anthology of writings by leading experts on the different aspects of suicide. One of the most widely respected overviews of the subject.

Prentice, Ann E. *Suicide*. Metuchen, N.J.: Scarecrow Press, 1974.

General overview of the subject.

Rauscher, William V. *The Case Against Suicide*. New York: St. Martin's Press, 1981.

Arguments against the toleration or acceptance of self-destruction.

Richman, Joseph. *Family Therapy for Suicidal People.* New York: Springer Publishing Co., 1986.

Explores the use of family counseling and therapy for suicidal people, describes the qualifications of an effective counselor, and discusses therapy techniques.

Seward, Jack. *Hara-Kiri: Japanese Ritual Suicide.* Rutland, Vermont: Charles F. Tuttle, 1968.

A history of hara-kiri, or Japanese ritual suicide.

Sexton, Anne. *Live or Die.* Boston: Houghton Mifflin, 1966.

Describes the poet's fascination and preoccupation with death. Sexton committed suicide in 1974.

Shneidman, Edwin S. *Voices of Death.* New York: Harper & Row, 1980; Bantam, 1982.

An analysis of suicidal motivations.

———*Death of Man.* New York: Jason Aronson, 1983.

Broad examination of suicide first published in 1973.

———*Definition of Suicide.* New York: John Wiley & Sons, 1985.

Overview of the subject by the founder of the American Association of Suicidology. Addresses the major aspects of suicide and includes a theoretical treatment of self-destructive behavior.

Shneidman, Edwin S., ed. *Essays in Self-Destruction.* New York: Jason Aronson, 1967.

Highly regarded anthology of writings on suicide.

———*Suicidology: Contemporary Developments.* New York: Grune and Stratton, 1976.

Anthology on developments in suicide studies.

Shneidman, Edwin S., and N. L. Farberow. *Clues to Suicide.* New York: McGraw-Hill, 1957.

Early work on suicide warning signs by two leading authorities.

Shneidman, Edwin S., Norman L. Farberow, and Robert E. Litman, eds. *The Psychology of Suicide.* New York: Science House, 1970.

Collection of writings on the psychodynamics of self-destructive behavior.

Stengel, Erwin. *Suicide and Attempted Suicide*, rev. ed. New York: Jason Aronson, 1974.

Major work by the preeminent British suicidologist. Emphasizes the important distinctions between suicide attempts and suicide completions. First published in 1964.

Varah, Chad. *The Samaritans: To Help Those Tempted to Suicide or Despair*. New York: Macmillan, 1966.

An account by its founder of the international organization dedicated to befriending the suicidal.

Wechsler, James A. *In a Darkness*. New York: W. W. Norton, 1972.

A book about the years of mental illness and suicide of the author's son, Michael.

Weisman, Avery, and Robert Kastenbaum. *The Psychological Autopsy: A Study of the Terminal Phase of Life*. New York: Behavorial Publications, 1968.

Describes the psychological autopsy.

Yourcenar, Marguerite. *Mishima: A Vision of the Void*. New York: Farrar, Straus & Giroux, 1986.

Account of the Japanese writer and his dramatic public *seppuka* in 1970.

YOUTH SUICIDE

Asinof, Eliot. *Craig and Joan*. New York: Viking Press, 1971.

The story of two New Jersey teens who killed themselves in 1969 to protest the Vietnam war.

Bolton, Iris. *My Son . . . My Son: A Guide to Healing After Death*. Atlanta: Boston Press, 1983.

A mother recounts her struggle to cope with her son's suicide.

Curran, David K. *Adolescent Suicidal Behavior*. New York: Hemisphere Publishing Corp., 1987.

Comprehensive review of research on teen suicide for professionals, parents, and others involved with young people.

Davis, Patricia A. *Suicidal Adolescents*. Springfield, Ill.: Charles C. Thomas, 1983.

Examines over 100 psychological studies of adolescent suicide. Chapters range from motivation and etiology to treatment and postvention.

Annotated Bibliography

Francis, Dorothy B. *Suicide: A Preventable Tragedy*. New York: Lodestar Books, 1989.

Examines historical attitudes toward self-destruction, profiles teenagers who have considered or attempted suicide, and explores present-day controversies in suicide education. Offers counsel to those who wish to help suicidal people.

Gardner, Sandra, and Gary Rosenberg. *Teenage Suicide*. New York: Julian Messner, 1986.

Describes causes, effects, behavior patterns, danger signals, and preventive measures. Also contains the stories of six young adults who tried to commit suicide.

Giffin, Mary, and Carol Felsenthal. *A Cry for Help: Exploring and Exploding the Myths about Teenage Suicide—A Guide for All Parents of Adolescents*. Garden City, N.Y.: Doubleday, 1983.

Directed to parents of young adults, the book discusses the many aspects of the phenomenon of teen suicide.

Hafen, Brent Q., and Kathryn J. Frandsen. *Youth Suicide: Depression and Loneliness*. Evergreen, Colorado: Cordillera Press, 1986.

Examines the contemporary phenomenon of youth suicide: risk factors, warning signs, preventive measures, and misconceptions.

Joan, Polly. *Preventing Teenage Suicide: The Living Alternative Handbook*. New York: Human Sciences Press, 1985.

Covers suicide dynamics, causes, warning signs, and intervention procedures.

Killinger, John. *The Loneliness of Children*. New York: Vanguard, 1980.

Argues that a lack of proper parental care and attention can lead to despair and even suicide. Suggests that problems arise when parents choose between their own needs and those of their children.

Klagsbrun, Francine. *Too Young to Die: Youth and Suicide*. New York: Pocket Books, 1985.

Combines the latest scientific research with case histories of young people who have attempted suicide. Includes guidance on how to deal with a suicidal person during a crisis and an annotated bibliography.

Kolehmainen, Janet, and Sandra Handwerk. *Teen Suicide: A Book for Friends, Family, and Classmates*. Minneapolis: Lerner Publications, 1986.

Written for the potential suicide victim's friends, classmates, and family. Describes the warning signs, causes, and myths.

Langone, John. *Dead End: A Book about Suicide*. Boston: Little, Brown, 1986.

Written for teens, parents, and those who work with youngsters. Discusses historical attitudes toward suicide, describes the psychological profile of suicide victims, and suggests ways to help those considering taking their own lives.

Leder, Jane Mersky. *Dead Serious: A Book for Teenagers About Teenage Suicide*. New York: Macmillan, 1987.

Provides information concerning factors, warning signs, and places to receive help. Case histories and interviews with teens who have attempted suicide are also included.

Mack, John E., and Holly Hickler. *Vivienne: The Life and Suicide of an Adolescent Girl*. New York: New American Library, 1982.

Examines the life and death of Vivienne Loomis, a 14-year-old girl who committed suicide on December 21, 1973, drawing on the letters, poetry, and journals she left behind. Also provides an introduction to the challenges facing youth in today's society. Includes a review of the current literature on adolescent suicide.

Madison, Arnold. *Suicide and Young People*. New York: Houghton-Mifflin/Clarion, 1978.

Focuses on the phenomenon in a worldwide context.

Peck, Michael L., Michael L. Farberow, and Robert E. Litman, eds. *Youth Suicide*. New York: Springer Publishing Co., 1985.

This work originated from a 1980 National Institute of Mental Health conference. Addresses psychodynamic issues in youth suicide, treatment strategies, and prevention measures.

Pfeffer, Cynthia R. *The Suicidal Child*. New York: Guilford Press, 1986.

Examines the research, theory, and treatment of suicidal behavior in children. A comprehensive list of references is included.

Rabkin, Brenda. *Growing Up Dead: A Hard Look at Why Adolescents Commit Suicide*. Nashville: Abingdon, 1979.

Reviews the causes of youth suicide.

Shneidman, Edwin S., ed. *Death and the College Student*. New York: Human Sciences Press, 1972.

Essays about suicide among Harvard University students.

Smith, Judie. *Coping with Suicide*. New York: Rosen Publishing Group, 1986.

A book about teenage suicide; the reasons, the signs to watch for, the importance of communication, and the ways that survivors can deal with grief.

Wrobleski, Adina. *Suicide: Why?: 85 Questions and Answers About Suicide*. Minneapolis: author, 1989.

Written in a question-and-answer format, this work gives advice for dealing with teens who exhibit suicidal behavior.

EUTHANASIA

Barnard, Christiaan. *Good Life, Good Death*. Englewood Cliffs, N.J.: Prentice-Hall, 1980.

Arguments for euthanasia by the noted heart surgeon. Supports the involvement of doctors in the practice.

Fletcher, Joseph. *Morals and Medicine*. Boston: Beacon Press, 1954.

An early plea for the legislation of euthanasia by the noted ethicist and theologian.

Humphry, Derek. *Let Me Die Before I Wake*. Los Angeles: Hemlock Society, 1984.

A defense of euthanasia and the right to "self-deliverance" for the terminally ill.

Humphry, Derek, and Ann Wickett. *Jean's Way*. New York: Quartet Books, 1978.

Recounts how Humphry helped his first wife, Jean, who was suffering from incurable cancer, to commit suicide.

————*The Right to Die: Understanding Euthanasia*. New York: Harper & Row, 1986.

An explanation of their advocacy of "rational voluntary euthanasia" by the husband and wife cofounders of the Hemlock Society.

Maguire, Daniel C. *Death by Choice*. New York: Doubleday, 1973.

A Roman Catholic theologian examines the question of death by choice in a medical context.

More, Thomas. *Utopia*. New York: Penguin Books, 1965.

Famous blueprint for a better world by the 16th-century theologian and thinker. More allowed for euthanasia in his hypothetical society. First published in 1551.

Portwood, Doris. *Common Sense Suicide: The Final Right*. New York: Dodd, Mead, 1978.

The author promotes a reappraisal of current thought on elderly suicide.

Rachels, James. *The End of Life: Euthanasia and Mortality*. New York: Oxford University Press, 1986.

Examines a person's right to die and the issues involved.

Rollin, Betty. *Last Wish*. New York: Lincoln Press/Simon and Schuster, 1985.

Describes how the author helped her terminally ill mother take her own life.

Roman, Jo. *Exit House: Choosing Suicide as an Alternative*. New York: Seaview Books, 1980.

Posthumously published account of the author's reasons for committing suicide. Offers a strong defense of euthanasia.

Szasz, Thomas. *Law, Liberty and Psychiatry: An Inquiry into the Social Uses of Mental Health Practices*. New York: Collier, 1968.

Dr. Szasz argues that an individual has a right to commit suicide. He opposes forced treatment and involuntary hospitalization for suicidal persons.

FICTION

Calvert, Patricia. *Hour of the Wolf*. New York: Macmillan, 1983.

Novel about a young man dealing with the suicide of a friend.

Ferris, Jean. *Amen, Moses Gardenia*. New York: Farrar, Straus and Giroux, 1983.

A 15-year-old girl has difficulties fitting into her new school. Her depression worsens when she has problems with her boyfriend. She then tries to end the isolation and pain.

Goethe, Johann Wolfgang von. *The Sorrows of Young Werther*. New York: Random House, 1971.

Romantic novel about a young man who commits suicide. The book had a strong influence on young people at the time it was first written in 1774.

Guest, Judith. *Ordinary People*. New York: Viking, 1976.

Novel about youth suicide that became the award-winning film of the same name.

Luger, Harriet. *Lauren*. New York: Dell, 1981.

Confronted by an unwanted pregnancy, a young woman considers suicide.

Miklowitz, Gloria D. *Close to the Edge*. New York: Dell, 1984.

A high school senior is thrown by the suicide of a friend.

O'Neal, Zibby. *A Formal Feeling*. New York: Viking-Penguin, 1982.

A young woman has difficulties coming to terms with the death of her mother.

Peck, Richard. *Remembering the Good Times*. New York: Delacorte Press, 1985.

Novel about a suicide among three teenage friends, and how the two survivors react.

ENCYCLOPEDIAS

"Depression," in *The World Book Encyclopedia*, vol. 5, 1988, 158.

Discusses mental depression as a major cause of suicide.

"Euthanasia," in *The Guide to American Law*, vol. 5, 1984, 23–24.

Examines the legal aspects and implications of euthanasia, or mercy killing. Outlines significant court cases.

"Emile Durkheim," in *The New Encyclopaedia Britannica*, 15th ed., vol. 4, 1985, 294–295.

A biographical sketch of French sociologist Emile Durkheim, with a discussion of his landmark study of suicide.

"Insurance," in *The New Encyclopaedia Britannica*, 15th ed. vol. 21, 1985, 678–691.

Briefly reviews the issue of insurance claims in suicide cases.

"Medical Disorders and Their Treatment," in *The New Encyclopaedia Britannica*, 15th ed., vol. 23, 1985, 956–975.

Discusses the depressive mental condition as the leading cause of suicide.

"Philosophies of the Branches of Knowledge," in *The New Encyclopaedia Britannica*, 15th ed., vol. 25, 1985, 669–741.

Contains a brief review of French writer and philosopher Jean Paul Sartre's work on suicide.

"Social Differentiation," in *The New Encyclopaedia Britannica*, 15th ed., vol. 27, 1985, 312–364.

Describes the high rate of suicide among the elderly, especially in the 19th and 20th centuries.

"Suicide," in *Academic American Encyclopedia*, vol. 18, 1988, 330–331.

Overview of the issue by Jack D. Douglas, author of *The Social Meanings of Suicide*. Addresses societal differences, statistical problems, types of suicide, and explanatory theories.

"Suicide," in *The Encyclopedia Americana International Edition*, vol. 18, 1988, 857–858.

Overview by the sociologist Ruth S. Cavan, author of *Suicide*. Examines modern concepts and factors influencing self-destructive behavior.

"Suicide," in *The Guide to American Law*, vol. 9, 1984, 429.

Defines suicide in the context of the law.

"Suicide," in *The New Encyclopaedia Britannica*, Micropedia, vol. 11, 1987, 359.

Outlines the historical context and discusses current thinking on suicide.

"Suicide," in *The World Book Encyclopedia*, vol. 18, 1988, 964.

Briefly outlines the history of suicide.

PERIODICALS

Concern for Dying. New York: Education Council for the Living Will (quarterly).

Newsletter of the education and public awareness organization Concern for Dying. Reports on developments concerning the living will, the right to die, and related issues.

Crisis: International Journal of Suicide and Crisis Studies. Toronto: C. J. Hogrefe (semiannual).

Professional journal on international research and developments in suicidology.

Hemlock Quarterly. Los Angeles: Hemlock Society (quarterly).

Reports on developments in voluntary euthanasia, the right to die, and related issues.

Monthly Vital Statistics Report. Washington, D.C.: National Center for Health Statistics (monthly).

Reports on the rate and incidence of suicide in the United States.

Newsletter (Society for the Right to Die). New York: Society for the Right to Die (quarterly).

Newsletter of the advocacy and education organization Society for the Right to Die. Reports on legislation, court cases, and other activities related to passive euthanasia and the right to die.

Newslink. Denver: American Association of Suicidology (quarterly).

Reports on current activities and developments in the suicide prevention field.

Omega. Farmingdale, N.Y.: Baywood Publishing Co. (quarterly).

Serves as an international forum on thanatology. Articles address terminal illness, suicide, bereavement and guilt, and related issues of death and dying.

Suicide and Life-Threatening Behavior. New York: Human Sciences Press (quarterly).

Professional journal on suicidology. Contains research, articles, and reviews.

Vital Statistics of the United States, Volume II, Mortality. Washington, D.C.: National Center for Health Statistics (annual).

Annual report on the rate and incidence of suicide in the United States.

The following periodicals frequently contain articles and information on suicide:

Alcohol Health and Research World. Rockville, Maryland: National Clearinghouse for Alcohol Information (quarterly).

American Journal of Drug and Alcohol Abuse. New York: Marcel Dekker (quarterly).

American Journal of Epidemiology. Baltimore: American Journal of Epidemiology (monthly).

American Journal of Pharmacy and the Sciences Supporting Public Health. Philadelphia: American Journal of Pharmacy (quarterly).

American Journal of Psychiatry. Washington, D.C.: American Psychiatric Association (monthly).

American Journal of Psychology. Champaign, Illinois: University of Illinois Press (quarterly).

American Journal of Public Health. Washington, D.C.: American Public Health Association (monthly).

American Journal of Sociology. Chicago: University of Chicago Press (bimonthly).

Annals of Internal Medicine. Philadelphia: American College of Physicians (monthly).

Archives of General Psychiatry. Chicago: American Medical Association (monthly).

British Medical Journal. London: British Medical Association (quarterly).

Contemporary Drug Problems. New York: Federal Legal Publications (quarterly).

Crime and Deliquency. Hackensack, N.J.: National Council on Crime and Deliquency (quarterly).

Criminology. Columbus, Ohio: American Society of Criminology (quarterly).

Digest of Addiction Theory and Application. Minneapolis: Johnson Institute (quarterly).

Drug Abuse and Alcoholism Newsletter. San Diego: Vista Hill Foundation (irregular).

Journal of Abnormal Psychology. Arlington, Virginia: American Psychological Association (quarterly).

Journal of Clinical Psychology. Brandon, Vermont: Clinical Psychology Publishing Co. (bimonthly).

Journal of Consulting and Clinical Psychology. Arlington, Virginia: American Psychological Association (bimonthly).

Journal of Criminal Law and Criminology. Chicago: Northwestern University School of Law (quarterly).

Journal of Drug Education. Farmingdale, N.Y.: Baywood Publishing Co. (quarterly).

Journal of Drug Issues. Tallahasse: Journal of Drug Issues (quarterly).

Journal of General Psychology. Washington, D.C.: Heldref Publications (quarterly).

Journal of Health and Social Behavior. Washington, D.C.: American Sociological Association (quarterly).

Journal of Nervous and Mental Disease. Baltimore: Williams and Wilkins (monthly).

Journal of Personality. Durham, N.C.: Duke University Press (quarterly).

Journal of Personality and Social Psychology. Arlington, Virginia: American Psychological Association (monthly).

Journal of Pharmacology and Experimental Therapeutics. Baltimore: Williams and Wilkins (monthly).

Journal of Psychoactive Drugs. New Brunswick, N.J.: Transaction Periodicals Consortium (quarterly).

Journal of Studies on Alcohol. Piscataway, N.J.: Alcohol Research Documentation (bimonthly).

Journal of the American Medical Association (JAMA). Chicago: American Medical Association (weekly).

New England Journal of Medicine. Boston: Massachusetts Medical Society (weekly).

Psychiatry Digest. Northfield, Illinois: Medical Digest (quarterly).

Psychological Reports. Missoula, Montana: Southern University Press (bimonthly).

Psychology and Aging. Arlington, Virginia: American Psychological Association (quarterly).

Social Problems. Berkeley: University of California Press (irregular).

Sociology. Guilford, Conn.: Dushkin Publishing (annual).

Sociology and Social Research. Los Angeles: University of Southern California (quarterly).

ARTICLES

GENERAL

Adams, K. S., A. Bouckoms, and C. Streiner. "Parental Loss and Family Stability in Attempted Suicide." *Archives of General Psychiatry* 39 (1982): 1081–1085.

Discusses the relationship between suicide and parental loss.

Alanen, Y. O., R. Rinne, and P. Paukkonen. "On Family Dynamics and Family Therapy in Suicidal Attempts." *Crisis* 2 (1981): 20–26.

A look at family dynamics and therapy in suicidal attempts.

Aldridge, D. "Family Interaction and Suicidal Behaviour: A Brief Review." *Journal of Family Therapy* 6 (1984): 309–322.

Examines the connection between family interaction and suicide risk.

Baker, Sherry. "Born Under a Bad Sign." *Omni*, November 1988, 26–28.

Looks at the possible link between traumatic birth experiences and suicides.

Barrett, William P. "Epitaph for a Trader." *Forbes*, December 14, 1987, 121.

Describes the life and death of John Markle.

Beard, Lillian. "Why Kids Die." *NEA Today*, November 1989, 15.

Written in question-and-answer format, this article explores suicide among children and young adults. Touches on cluster suicides and warning signs. Gives suggestions for friends or teachers who are approached by someone who may be suicidal.

Bedeian, A. G. "Suicide and Occupation: A Review." *Journal of Vocational Behavior* 21 (1982): 206–223.

Reviews the literature on the relationship between suicide and various occupations.

Annotated Bibliography

Bell, Alison. "Bummer Blues." *Teen Magazine*, April 1987, 100–101.

Discusses teen depression for a teen audience.

Berger, Paula S. "Teaching About Teen Suicide Using Young-Adult Novels." *Education Digest*, April 1987, 48–49.

Suggests that teens may investigate the topic of suicide through novels that have depicted it. Advises that teachers receive training on suicide prevention.

Bollen, K. A., and D. P. Phillips. "Imitative Suicides: A National Study of the Effects of Television News Stories," *American Sociological Review* 47 (1982): 802–809.

Explores the link between television stories on suicides and the suicide rate.

Bordewich, Fergus M. "Mortal Fears." *The Atlantic*, February 1988, 30–34.

Discusses the fact that only recently have schools begun to offer courses on death and dying.

Bouvier, L. F. "America's Baby Boom Generation: The Fateful Bulge." *Population Bulletin* 35 (1980): 1–35.

Describes the baby boom generation and suicide rates.

Brower, Montgomery. "Lost Too Soon." *People Weekly*, May 21, 1990, 56–60.

Describes teen suicides in Sheridan, Arkansas.

Cohen-Sandler, R., A. Berman, and R. King. "Suicidal Behavior in Children and Early Adolescence." *Journal of the American Academy of Child Psychiatry* 21 (1982): 178–186.

Explores suicidal behavior in young adults and children.

"Crise du Jour." *National Review*, May 8, 1987, 19–21.

Describes government policy and teenage suicide.

Dismuke, Diane. "Reducing Suicides." *NEA Today*, November 1988, 21.

Discusses the student suicide rate and suggests ways of reducing it. Includes a ten-point set of recommendations on planning community action.

Eckman, Fern Marja. "Teen Suicide." *McCall's*, October 1987, 71–74.

Provides an overview of teen suicides—personal cases, symptoms, where to obtain assistance. Written for parents, the article suggests ways to communicate without alienating teens.

"The Ecology of Suicide." *National Review*, April 24, 1987, 18–19.

Discusses the current "wave of concern" that follows suicides, including "bizarre local incidents, massive publicity, statistic-laden experts, concerned editorials, and legislators climbing over one another to fund new state and federal programs."

Edwards, Thomas K. "Giving Students Reasons for Wanting to Live." *Education Digest*, March 1989, 22–24.

Written for the secondary school teacher, the article focuses on "mentoring" or "advising" students to foster their academic and personal growth.

Elkind, David. "The Facts About Teen Suicide." *Parents' Magazine*, January 1990, 111.

Provides information on suicides of adolescents. Describes warning signs and suggests ideas for parents who have a child in crisis.

"An Enigma of Youth: Suicide." *The Economist*, March 21, 1987, 28–29.

A short overview of recent teen suicide attempts beginning with the New Jersey quadruple suicide and how it may have influenced attempts across the country. Explores current speculation about why teenage suicide is on the rise: the decline of the church, the divorce rate, and poverty.

Eskin, Leah, with Debbie Thunder. "Teens Take Charge." *Scholastic Update*, May 26, 1989, 26–27.

Following a suicide epidemic at the Wind River Reservation in Wyoming, students banded together to try to help others take control of their lives.

Farberow, Norman, and E. Shneidman. "Attempted, Threatened and Completed Suicide." *Journal of Abnormal Social Psychiatry* 50 (1955): 230.

A comprehensive look at suicide.

Forliti, John E. "You're a Mess, Allie—But the Banquet's Ready." *National Catholic Reporter*, October 21, 1988, 9.

Presents a funeral homily for a suicide victim.

Frymier, Jack. "Understanding and Preventing Teen Suicide: An Interview with Barry Garfinkel." *Phi Delta Kappan*, December 1988, 290–293.

The number of teens in the United States who kill themselves has increased 300% in the last 30 years. Dr. Barry Garfinkel, an authority on child and adolescent suicide, explores appropriate responses by the schools to suicide.

Gispert, Maria, Kirk Wheeler, Loralee Marsh, and Maryellen S. Davis. "Suicidal Adolescents: Factors in Evaluation." *Adolescence*, Winter 1985, 753–762.

Discusses evaluative factors in suicidal youth.

Griffith, Ezra E. H., and Carl C. Bell. "Recent Trends in Suicide and Homicide Among Blacks." *Journal of the American Medical Association*, October 27, 1989, 2265–2270.

Discusses a recent study contrasting black and white suicide rates.

Harry, J. "Parasuicide, Gender, and Gender Deviance." *Journal of Health and Social Behavior* 24 (1983): 350–361.

Explores the interrelationship of suicide and homosexuality.

Hoagland, Edward. "The Urge for an End: Contemplating Suicide." *Harper's Magazine*, March 1988, 45–51.

Examines the process of contemplating suicide.

Holinger, P. C. "Adolescent Suicide: An Epidemiological Study of Recent Trends." *American Journal of Psychiatry* 135 (1987): 754–756.

Presents recent trends in adolescent suicides.

"I Wanted to Die." *Reader's Digest*, July 1987, 93–96. (part 1 of a series).

Talks about a young woman's suicide attempt as a senior in high school and the struggle and rebuilding of her life after the attempt. Suggests that those who are aware of potential suicide victims reach out and try to help.

Jacobs, Colleen, and Linda Moffatt. "My Baby Has Suffered Enough." *Woman's Day*, February 6, 1990, 76–81.

Describes the difficulties of making an agonizing decision whether to authorize surgery or let an infant die.

Jahr, Cliff. "Hollywood Scandals." *Cosmopolitan*, August 1988, 220–224.

Focuses on suicides by various famous actors and actresses.

Johnson, Barclay D. "Durkheim's One Cause of Suicide." *American Sociological Review*, December 1965, 875–886.

A study on Durkheim and suicide.

Karcher, Charles J., and Leonard L. Linden. "Is Work Conducive to Self-Destruction?" *Suicide and Life-Threatening Behavior*, Fall 1982, 151–195.

Reviews the possible connection between work and suicide.

Konopka, G. "Adolescent Suicide." *Exceptional Children* 49 (1983): 390–393.

An overview of teenage suicide.

Lester, D. "National Homicide and Suicide Rates as a Function of Political Stability." *Psychological Reports* 33 (1973): 298.

Outlines suicide and homicide rates and their relation to political stability.

Loo, Robert. "Suicide Among Police in a Federal Force." *Suicide and Life-Threatening Behavior*, Fall 1986, 3.

A study on federal police suicide rates.

Magnuson, Ed. "Suicides: The Gun Factor." *Time*, July 17, 1989, 61.

An analysis of suicides by guns.

Malinowski, B. "Suicide: A Chapter in Comparative Ethics." *Sociology Review* 1 (1908): 14.

Discusses suicide and ethics.

Maris, Ronald. "The Adolescent Suicide Problem." *Suicide and Life-Threatening Behavior* 15 (1985): 91–109.

Covers the increase of suicides among those aged 14 to 24 since the 1960s.

Martz, Larry, Peter McKillop, Andy Murr, and Ray Anello. "The Copycat Suicides." *Newsweek*, March 23, 1987, 28–29.

Describes teen death pacts in communities in New Jersey and Illinois. Examines fears of a copycat suicide epidemic.

Mohler, Mary. "Teen Suicide: The Sobering Facts." *Ladies Home Journal*, November 1987, 106–107.

A general discussion of the statistics on teen suicides. Gives warning signs of potential suicides.

Motto, Jerome. "Suicide Attempts: A Longitudinal View." *Archives of General Psychiatry* 13 (1965) 516–20.

Examines suicide attempts over a long period of time.

———"Newspaper Influence on Suicide: A Controlled Study." *Archives of General Psychiatry* 23 (1970): 143–148.

Explores the link between suicide rates and the press coverage of suicides.

Parsons, Richard D. "Postvention: Surviving Adolescent Suicide." *New Catholic World*, November-December 1987, 259–263.

Focuses on the family and friends left behind and how the grieving process differs from a nonsuicide death.

Peck, D. L. "Towards a Theory of Suicide: A Case for Modern Fatalism." *Omega* 11 (1980–81): 1–14.

Advances a theory of suicide in today's world.

Pierce, Albert. "The Economic Cycle and the Social Suicide Rate." *American Sociological Review*, June 1967, 427–462.

Examines the relationship of economic swings in fortune to the suicide rate.

Platt, S. "Unemployment and Suicidal Behaviour: A Review of the Literature." *Social Science and Medicine* 19 (1984):93–115.

A review of the literature on suicide and unemployment.

"Preventing Teenage Suicide." *The Futurist*, September-October 1987, 55–56.

Identifying risk factors for suicide attempts as the first step in a strategy of prevention.

Rich, C. L., R. C. Fowler, D. Young, and M. Blenkush. "San Diego Suicide Study: Comparison of Gay to Straight Males." *Suicide and Life-Threatening Behavior* 16 (1986): 448–457.

Compares suicide patterns among gay males and heterosexual men.

"Rock on Trial." *The Economist*, October 15, 1988, 38.

Describes a possible connection between rock music and suicide.

"Romeo and Juliet and Suicide." *USA Today*, December 1989, 15.

Uses lines from Shakespeare's tragedy *Romeo and Juliet* to educate parents about teenagers and suicide. An analysis of the quotes attempts to reveal warning signs and reasons why people commit suicide. Suggests ways parents or caretakers of teenagers can help.

Rosen, George. "History in the Study of Suicide." *Psychological Medicine: A Journal for Research in Psychiatry and the Allied Sciences* 1 (1971): 4.

Presents a historical view of suicide.

Salive, Marcel E., Gordon S. Smith, and Fordham Brewer. "Suicide Mortality in the Maryland State Prison System, 1979 through 1987." *Journal of the American Medical Association*, July 21, 1989, 365–369.

Describes the suicide rate in the Maryland state prison system.

Saunders, J. M., and S. M. Valente. "Suicide Risk Among Gay Men and Lesbians: A Review." *Death Studies* 11 (1986): 1–23.

Reviews a study of the risk of suicide among homosexuals.

Saxon, Wolfgang. "Edward Winter, 84; Had Sued Hospital For Saving His Life." *The New York Times*, April 17, 1990, A15ff.

Obituary of Edward Winter, 84, who took legal action when a nurse revived him rather than allow him to die.

Schwartz, A. "Inaccuracy and Uncertainty in Estimates of College Student Suicide Rates." *Journal of the American College Health Association* 28 (1980): 201–204.

A study of suicide rates among college students.

Seibel, Maxine, and Joseph N. Murray. "Early Prevention of Adolescent Suicide." *Education Digest*, November 1988, 30–32.

Explores the concept of a team approach to preventing teen suicide.

Seiden, Richard H. "Campus Tragedy: A Study of Student Suicides." *Journal of Abnormal Psychology* 3 (1966): 285–289.

Discusses the rate and occurrance of campus suicides.

————"We're Driving Young Blacks to Suicide." *Psychology Today*, August 1970, 24–28.

Presents a study of black suicide.

Shaffer, D., A. Garland, M. Gould, P. Fisher, and P. Trautman. "Preventing Teenage Suicide: A Critical Review." *Journal of the American Academy of Child and Adolescent Psychiatry* 27 (1988): 675–687.

Reviews prevention strategies for teenage suicide.

Shamoo, Tonia K., and Philip G. Petros. "Suicide Intervention Strategies for the Adolescent." *Techniques*, April 1985, 297–303.

Discusses intervention strategies for teens at risk of commiting suicide.

Shapiro, Joseph P. "Larry McAfee, Invisible Man." *U.S. News & World Report*, February 19, 1990, 59–60.

A motorcycle accident left Larry McAfee unable to move any muscle below his chin. Shuffled from hospital to hospital, he wants to be able to take his own life. He says that since he became disabled, attendants act as if he has lost the right to make decisions.

Shneidman, E. S. "Preventing Suicide." *American Journal of Nursing*, May 1965, 111–116.

Discusses ways for hospital staff and laypersons to prevent suicide.

Simmons, Kathryn. "Task Force to Make Recommendations for Adolescents in Terms of Suicide Risk." *Journal of the American Medical Association*, June 26, 1987, 3330–3332.

Describes the work of the task force that studied the suicide risk of adolescents.

Sloan, John Henry, Frederick P. Rivara, Donald T. Reay, James A. J. Ferris, and Arthur L. Kellermann. "Firearm Regulations and Rates of Suicides." *New England Journal of Medicine*, February 8, 1990, 369–373.

Investigates the theory that gun control may reduce the incidence of suicide. Firearms are involved in 57% of suicides in the United States.

Smith, K., and S. Crawford. "Suicidal Behaviors Among 'Normal' High School Students." *Suicide and Life-Threatening Behavior* 16 (1986): 313–325.

Examines suicide among those teens thought not to be at risk.

Smith, K., and R. Maris. "Suggested Recommendations for the Study of Suicide and Other Life-Threatening Behaviors." *Suicide and Life-Threatening Behavior* 16 (1986): 67–69.

Outlines recommendations for the study of suicide.

Smith, Richard D. "Too Sad to Live, Too Young to Die." *American Legion Magazine* (March 1987): 32.

Explores suicides among teenagers.

Stack, S. "The Effect of Strikes on Suicide: A Cross-National Analysis. *Sociological Focus* 15 (1982): 135–146.

Explores the impact of labor strikes on suicidal behavior.

———"A Leveling Off in Young Suicides." *The Wall Street Journal*, May 28, 1986, 34.

Presents figures on dropping suicide rates among adolescents.

Stupple, Donna-Marie. "Rx for the Suicide Epidemic." *English Journal*, January 1987, 64–70.

Describes patterns of suicidal behavior among young people.

Teicher, J. D. "Children and Adolescents Who Attempt Suicide." *Pediatric Clinics of North America* 17 (1970): 687–696.

Explores the suicides of children and young adults.

Weiss, R. "Teen Suicide Clusters: More than Mimicry." *Science News*, November 25, 1989, 342.

Reports on the first study to look at teenage suicide clusters. This study of two Texas clusters shows that teenagers who commited suicide had no more exposure to other suicides than the control group.

Westermarck, E. "Suicide: A Chapter in Comparative Ethics." *Sociological Review* 1 (1908):12–33.

Presents a study in comparative ethics and suicide.

White, Wendy. "Teen Suicide: When Living Hurts." *Teen Magazine*, January 1988, 70–72.

Focuses on suicide warning signs and causative factors. Gives suggestions on what to do when confronted with a person who is contemplating suicide.

Wilentz, Amy. "Teen Suicide: Two Death Pacts Shake the Country." *Time*, March 23, 1987, 12–13.

Tells the story of four Bergenfield, N.J., youths who made a death pact and commited suicide.

Witkin, Gordon. "Groping to Cope with Teen Suicide: Communities Respond." *U.S. News & World Report*, March 30, 1987, 12.

Discusses "copycat" teen deaths. Suggests that teens most likely to commit suicide will not go through the traditional help channels—schools, mental health centers, and telephone hot lines.

Wolfle, Jane. "Adolescent Suicide—An Open Letter to Counselors: The Mother of a Suicide Victim Speaks Out." *Phi Delta Kappan*, December 1988, 294–295.

This open letter to counselors details the events that led up to Wolfe's son's death. It suggests that counselors inform parents when their children talk about commiting suicide.

Wrobleski, A. "The Suicide Survivors Grief Group." *Omega* 15 (1984–85): 173–184.

Explores methods used by those in a suicide survivors grief group.

"Youth Suicide—United States, 1970–1980." *Journal of the American Medical Association*, June 16, 1987, 3333–3335.

Presents information on youth suicides during the 1970s.

Zilboorg, G. "Considerations on Suicide." *American Journal of Orthopsychiatry* 15 (1945): 31.

Discusses the various aspects of suicide.

———"Suicide Among Civilized and Primitive Roles." *American Journal of Psychiatry* 92 (1936): 1347–1369.

Examines suicide among civilized and primitive cultures.

LEGAL

Butler, Mary S. "Answers to Your Most-Asked Legal Questions." *Consumers Digest*, March/April 1988, 73–78.

Furnishes answers to frequently asked questions on living wills.

Cahalan, Kathleen A. "Living Wills: Speak Now and Forever Rest In Peace." *U.S. Catholic*, January 1990, 25–30.

Defines a living will and describes how it helps ease the decision on whether to prolong medical treatment.

Carey, Joseph. "The Faulty Promise of 'Living Wills.' " *U.S. News & World Report*, July 24, 1989, 63–65.

Describes the problems raised by living wills for the medical profession.

Davidson, Kent W., Chris Hackler, Debra R. Caradine, and Ronald S. McCord. "Physicians' Attitudes on Advance Directives." *Journal of the American Medical Association*, November 3, 1989, 2415–2419.

Discusses advance directives, such as living wills and durable powers of attorney.

"Death Wish." *Time*, September 18, 1989, 67.

Describes Larry McAfee, a quadriplegic who successfully petitioned a Georgia court to allow him to take his own life. Reviews some of the arguments of disability rights activists.

Drinan, Robert F. "The Right to Die Reaches the U.S. Supreme Court." *America*. January 27, 1990, 60–61.

Depicts the case of *Cruzan v. Harmon*, in which the victim's parents are seeking permission to allow their comatose daughter, Nancy, to die.

Greene, Michelle, and Meg Grant. "A Florida Jury Finds No Guilt in Physician Peter Rosier's Fatal Devotion to His Dying Wife." *People*, December 19, 1988, 121ff.

The story of Patricia Rosier, 43, who, with the help of her pathologist husband, Peter, tried to commit suicide by overdose. When she did not die, Peter administered morphine and her father smothered her.

Kinsley, Michael. "To Be or Not to Be." *The New Republic*, November 27, 1989, 6ff.

Explores the Constitution's place in the current right-to-die argument. Kinsley states that the real question is not about the right to die but about the "right to refuse medical treatment." Also discusses the case of Nancy Beth Cruzan.

McKown, Delos B. "Demythologizing Natural Human Rights." *The Humanist*, May/June 1989, 21–29.

Describes the constitutional questions framed by the right-to-die issue.

MEDICAL

Adams, Charles G. "Should a Doctor Help His Patient Commit Suicide?" *Jet*, April 24, 1989, 14.

The author asks, "Is it ethically or morally wrong for a physician to help a hopelessly ill patient commit suicide?" and looks at this question from the vantage point of the black community.

Botkin, Jeffrey R., and S. Van McCrary. "Hospital Policy on Advance Directives: Do Institutions Ask Patients About Living Wills?" *Journal of the American Medical Association*, November 3, 1989, 2411–2414.

The authors completed a random survey of hospitals to see if they have policies on living wills or durable powers of attorney.

Colen, B. D. "Suicide Made Simple." *Health* (June 1988), 10ff.

Proposes that physicians should neither interfere with nor assist a terminally ill patient who tries to take his own life.

Davidson, Lucy E., Mark L. Rosenberg, James A. Mercy, Jack Franklin, and Jane T. Simmons. "An Epidemiologic Study of Risk Factors in Two Teenage Suicide Clusters." *Journal of the American Medical Association*, November 17, 1989, 2687–2692.

Annotated Bibliography

Suicide accounts for more than 6,000 deaths annually in the United States. Among young adults between the ages of 15 and 25, suicide ranks as the second leading cause of death. Often, many suicides occur in clusters within a single community.

Davis, F. B. "The Relationship Between Suicide and Attempted Suicide: A Review of the Literature." *Psychiatric Quarterly* 41 (1967): 752–765.

A study on the relationship of attempted to completed suicides.

Emanuel, Linda L., and Ezekiel J. Emanuel. "The Medical Directive: A New Comprehensive Advance Care Document." *Journal of the American Medical Association,* June 9, 1989, 3288–3393.

Focuses on the growth of living wills and the problems associated with them. Suggests application of a "Medical Directive" defining specific treatment and/or instructions by the patient to the physician in the case of terminal illness.

Folkenberg, Judy. "Suicide Chemistry." *American Health: Fitness of Body and Mind,* May 1989, 107.

Describes how low growth hormones may signal suicide risk.

Glass, Richard M. "AIDS and Suicide." *Journal of the American Medical Association,* March 4, 1988, 1368–1370.

An editorial on the tendency of AIDS patients to commit suicide.

Kessler, R. C., and J. A. MacRae, Jr. "Trends in the Relationship Between Sex and Attempted Suicide." *Journal of Health and Social Behavior* 24 (1983): 98–110.

Presents trends in the relationship between attempted suicide and gender.

Kolata, G. "Manic-Depression: Is It Inherited?" *Science,* May 2, 1986, 575.

Examines the genetic component in manic-depression.

Miles, Steven H., Peter A. Singer, and Mark Siegler. "Conflicts Between Patients' Wishes to Forgo Treatment and the Policies of Health Care Facilities." *New England Journal of Medicine,* July 5, 1989, 48–51.

Focuses on the conflicts between the policies of hospitals and other health care facilities and a patient's wish to die.

O'Brien, Marilyn. "Rebel with a Cause." *Health*, September 1987, 17.

Results of a ten-year study show that child and teen suicides stem from serious emotional problems and that the suicides are well thought out ahead of time.

Perry, Samuel, Lawrence Jacobsberg, and Baruch Fishman. "Suicidal Ideation and HIV Testing." *Journal of the American Medical Association*, February 2, 1990, 678–682.

Reports on studies that show a high incidence of suicide among AIDS-virus carriers.

"Persistent Vegetative State and the Decision to Withdraw or Withhold Life Support." *Journal of the American Medical Association*, January 19, 1990, 426–430.

Deciding when to withdraw life support measures for the terminally ill is an active public and legal debate. A report on the issue by the *JAMA* holds the physician must be the one to decide when there is virtually no chance of patient recovery. Provides the American Medical Association's definition of persistent vegetative state.

Pfeffer, Cynthia R. "Suicidal Fantasies in Normal Children." *Journal of Nervous and Mental Disease*, February 1985, 78–84.

Explores suicidal thoughts in young children.

Pokorny, Alex D. "Suicide Rates in Various Psychiatric Disorders." *Journal of Nervous and Mental Disorders* 139 (1964): 499–506.

Describes various psychiatric disorders and corresponding suicide rates.

Reich, Peter. "Panic Attacks and the Risk of Suicide." *New England Journal of Medicine*, November 2, 1989, 1260–1261.

Intense anxiety and fear comprise panic attacks. A study shows that the risk of suicide is higher for those patients suffering from panic disorders.

Robbins, Douglas R., and Norman E. Alessi. "Depressive Symptoms and Suicidal Behavior in Adolescents." *American Journal of Psychiatry*, May 1985, 588–592.

Discusses symptoms and suicidal behavior in teens.

Robins, E., et al. "The Communications of Suicidal Intent: A Study of 134 Consecutive Cases of Successful (Completed) Suicides." *American Journal of Psychiatry* 115 (1959) 724–733.

A study of the communication of suicide threats in 134 completed suicides.

Rotheram, M. J. "Evaluation of Imminent Danger for Suicide Among Youth." *American Journal of Orthopsychiatry* 57 (1987): 102–110.

Evaluates those factors that might put a youth at risk for suicide.

Roy, A. "Suicide in Depressives." *Comprehensive Psychiatry* 24 (1983): 487–491.

A clinical analysis of suicide among depressed people.

Roy, A., and M. Linnoila. "Alcoholism and Suicide." *Suicide and Life-Threatening Behavior* 16 (1986): 244–273.

Explores the connection between alcoholism and suicide.

Rudestam, K. E. "Physical and Psychological Responses to Suicide in the Family." *Journal of Consulting and Clinical Psychology* 45 (1977): 162–170.

Discusses the physical and psychological responses of family members to suicide.

Shafii, M., S. Carigan, J. R. Whittinghill, and A. Derrick. "Psychological Autopsy of Completed Suicide in Children and Adolescents." *American Journal of Psychiatry* 142 (1985): 1061–1064.

Reviews a psychological study of teenage and child suicides.

Wanzer, Sidney H., et al., "The Physician's Responsibility Toward Hopelessly Ill Patients: a Second Look." *New England Journal of Medicine*, March 30, 1989, 844–850.

Discusses popular attitudes about the rights of dying patients and addresses the physician's role in assisting a patient with suicide.

Wolfgang, Marvin. "An Analysis of Homicide-Suicide." *Journal of Clinical and Experimental Psychopathology* 19 (1958): 208–218.

Compares homicide and suicide patterns.

EUTHANASIA

Bloom, Mark. "Article Embroils JAMA in Ethical Controversy." *Science*, March 11, 1988, 1235–1236

Reviews the controversy over the article "It's Over, Debbie," published in the *Journal of the American Medical Association*. Probes such issues as the right to die, medical ethics, and the legality of euthanasia.

Boczkiewicz, Robert E. "Study Says Catholic Doctors Less Likely to Use Euthanasia." *National Catholic Reporter*, June 17, 1988, 24.

A Denver study of physicians and the use of euthanasia concluded that Catholic physicians in Colorado were less likely to aid in euthanasia than their Protestant or Jewish colleagues.

Burleigh, Michael. "Euthanasia and the Third Reich." *History Today*, February 1990, 22ff.

Describes how the Nazis twisted the debate over euthanasia and used it to rationalize a campaign of mass extermination.

Callahan, Daniel. "Vital Distinctions, Mortal Questions: Debating Euthanasia & Health Care Costs." *Commonweal*, July 15, 1988, 397–404.

Deals with the complicated issue of euthanasia and health care. Suggests the need to define what makes a society good and where the pursuit of health and the avoidance of death fit within society.

———"Euthanasia and Health-Care: Mortal Questions." *Current*, November 1988, 11–19.

Suggests several questions for consideration with euthanasia. Discusses growing support for active euthanasia and assisted suicide.

Colen, B. D. "The Extraordinary Case of the Woman Who Couldn't Die." *Redbook*, March 1989, 126ff.

The case of Nancy Jobes, a pregnant 24-year-old medical technician who was in a car accident that killed her fetus. When she was operated on to remove the fetus, her heart stopped temporarily and she suffered severe brain damage. The family requested euthanasia and pressed for legal permission in the courts.

de Wachter, M. A. M. "Active Euthanasia in the Netherlands." *Journal of the American Medical Association*, December 15, 1989, 3316–3319.

While mercy killing is a criminal offense in most countries, a 1973 Dutch court case allowed physicians to practice euthanasia under four conditions: incurable illness, unbearable suffering, the patient initiated the request, the patient's physician performs the euthanasia.

"Die as You Choose." *The Economist*, March 5, 1988, 13.

Focuses on a recent mercy killing and article on the incident in the *Journal of the American Medical Association*. Questions the assumption that all forms of mercy killing are wrong, citing examples of euthanasia in other countries.

Annotated Bibliography

"Feeling No Pain." *The New Republic*, November 27, 1989, 9–10.

Describes the right-to-die case of Nancy Cruzan, a terminally ill patient whose fate lies with the U.S. Supreme Court. Discusses living wills and who is authorized to make the decision on a patient's right to die.

Fenigsen, Richard. "Euthanasia: How It Works, the Dutch Experience." *Current*, June 1989, 4–14.

Dutch physicians perform 5,000 to 10,000 cases of euthanasia every year. Describes "voluntary" euthanasia in Holland and examines why it is rejected in the United States.

Ferrieri, Giuliano. "Death by Choice." *World Press Review*, December 1987, 51.

Describes the work of Dutch anesthesiologist Dr. Pieter Admiraal, a longtime advocate of euthanasia.

Gest, Ted, with Sarah Bruke. "Is There a Right to Die?" *U.S. News & World Report*, December 11, 1989, 35ff. 35–37.

Describes the Nancy Cruzan and Karen Ann Quinlan cases. Also discusses euthanasia and the elderly, and who should decide on euthanasia—a family member, physicians, or the government.

Gibbs, Nancy. "Love and Let Die." *Time*, March 19, 1990, 62–70.

Explores the Cruzan family's petition to the Supreme Court on the right to die. Also depicts other situations where either a terminally ill person would like the right to die or family members believe their relative would want to have the suffering end.

Goetz, Harriet. "Euthanasia: A Bedside View." *The Christian Century*, June 21–28, 1989, 619–622.

A nurse discusses the changes in attitudes toward euthanasia on the part of health care professionals.

Gotlieb, Anthony. "Learning How to Die: We Must Learn a Better Way of Death Before the Century Is Out." *The Economist Annual*. 1990, 23–24.

Examines the moral and ethical aspects of the right-to-die controversy.

Grady, Denise. "The Doctor Decided on Death: A Candid Tale of Mercy Killing Inflames the Profession." *Time*, February 15, 1988, 88.

A brief account of the mercy killing of a patient, Debbie, by a physician that inspired a huge debate in the medical and legal professions.

Grogan, David, and Jeanne Gordon. "The Founder of a 'Right to Die' Group Walks Out on His Wife When Cancer Threatens Her Life." *People*, March 12, 1990, 76–78.

Details the marital problems of the cofounders of the Hemlock Society and the impact of these difficulties on the right-to-die group.

Humphry, Derek. "Legislating for Active Voluntary Euthanasia." *The Humanist*, March/April 1988, 10ff.

Derek Humphry, founder and executive director of the Hemlock Society, discusses the legislative lobbying on euthanasia in California.

Kass, Leon R. "Death with Dignity & the Sanctity of Life." *Commentary*, March 1990, 33–43.

Explores the sanctity of life and human dignity in Judeo-Christian traditions and the Bible. Touches on the concept of "death with dignity" and concludes that euthanasia is "undignified and dangerous."

Kenkelen, Bill. "Euthanasia Backers Fail to Get Enough Signatures by Deadline." *National Catholic Reporter*, May 20, 1988, 2.

In California, lobbyists needed 400,000 signatures by May 6, 1988, to qualify for a state initiative on euthanasia backed by the Hemlock Society. Opponents of the initiative included the California Medical Association and the California Catholic Conference.

Klein, Robert J. "Why Everyone Should Write a Living Will." *Money*, June 1989, 165–166.

Stresses the need for everyone to have a living will.

Landos, John. "Baby Doe Five Years Later: Implications for Child Health." *New England Journal of Medicine*, August 13, 1987, 444–448.

Editorial discussing the legality and morality of passive euthanasia in the neonatal intensive care unit.

Levine, Carol. "God's Will Versus Doctor's Orders." *Parents' Magazine*, March 1989, 220–224.

Describes the care of sick children and their right to die. Also examines the moral and legal arguments involved.

Macklin, Ruth. "First Word." *Omni*, November 1988, 4.

The Hemlock Society, in favor of legalizing euthanasia, surveyed 5,000 physicians about their beliefs on mercy killing. Of the 588 respondents, 62% thought that it was "sometimes right" for physicians to assist the terminally ill who had asked to die.

Annotated Bibliography

Malcolm, Andrew H. "2 Right-to-Die Groups Merging for Unified Voice." *The New York Times*, April 12, 1990, A14ff.

Concern for Dying and the Society for the Right to Die are moving toward a merger. This is expected to create a unified lobbying and educational voice. The article also explores the change in attitude toward living wills, with more states now legally recognizing them.

Marx, Linda. "The Agony Did Not End for Roswell Gilbert, Who Killed His Wife to Give Her Peace." *People Weekly*, January 12, 1987, 30–35.

In 1985 Roswell Gilbert shot his wife, Emily, to end her suffering from Alzheimer's disease and osteoporosis, a degenerative bone disease. Gilbert was sentenced to life imprisonment for murder.

Oliwenstein, Lori. "It's Over, Debbie." *Discover*, January 1989, 80–81.

Describes the death of the terminally ill patient, Debbie, whose physician administered morphine to kill her. This event was reported in the *Journal of the American Medical Association* and caused a debate throughout the medical and legal professions.

Orntlicher, David. "Physician Participation in Assisted Suicide." *Journal of the American Medical Association*, October 6, 1988, 1844–1846.

Describes a recent study by the *New England Journal of Medicine* on a panel of physicians who, when asked whether physicians should help patients commit suicide if they were terminally ill, overwhelmingly said yes.

Relin, David Oliver. "Between Life and Death." *Scholastic Update*, January 26, 1990, 20–22.

Discusses the Nancy Cruzan right-to-die case. Notes that the Cruzans are not the only ones to be put in a position of deciding on euthanasia. Cites American Medical Association estimates that 70% of the population will have to face this question because of the advances in medical technology and treatment.

Rosenfeld, Albert. "Tough Cases, Hard Choices." *New York*, January 9, 1989, 3237.

Describes the difficult issues raised in several recent euthanasia cases.

Scully, Thomas and Celia Scully. "Playing God." *Glamour*, January 1988, 78ff.

Relates several stories of family members faced with making a decision on euthanasia. The authors recommend that one get as much information as possible from doctors, family members, and friends before making any decisions.

Schmidt, Stephen. "Living with Chronic Illness: Why Should I Go On?" *The Christian Century*, May 3, 1989, 475–479.

Describes chronic illness and the moral and religious aspects of the right to die.

Starr, Mark. "Prayer in the Courtroom: When Does Christian Science Become a Crime?" *Newsweek*, April 30, 1990, 64.

Explores the question of the right of a patient to refuse medical treatment. Examines legal and moral implications and how they apply to Christian Scientists.

Stout, Kate. "I Want to Die." *McCall's*, September 1988, 105–108.

The story of Clifford Culham, 57, who chose to die rather than suffer further with Lou Gehrig's disease. Recounts his struggle and his family's coming to grips with his decision.

Wolinsky, Anja. "Euthanasia." *The Humanist*, January/February 1988, 24ff.

The author writes that society must work to "implement the humanitarian benefits of death with dignity while minimizing the potential for abuse." She questions whether euthanasia is wrong if it "is the only way of relieving suffering."

GOVERNMENT DOCUMENTS

Allison, Margaret, Robert L. Hubbard, and Harold M. Ginzburg. *Indicators of Suicide and Depression Among Drug Abusers*. Rockville, Md.: National Institute on Drug Abuse, Division of Clinical Research, 1985.

Research monograph on indicators of suicidal proclivities among drug abusers.

————*Suicide and Depression Among Drug Abusers*. Rockville, Md.: National Institute on Drug Abuse, Division of Clinical Research, 1985.

Findings of research on patterns of suicide and depression among drug abusers.

Centers for Disease Control. *Suicide Surveillance: Summary 1970–1980*. Atlanta: Center for Health Promotion and Education, 1985.

A summary report and statistical picture of suicide in the United States in the 1970s.

Annotated Bibliography

Feinleib, Marcia R. *Report of the Secretary's Task Force on Youth Suicide.* 4 vs. Rockville, Md.: U.S. Dept. of Health and Human Services, Public Health Service, Alcohol, Drug Abuse, and Mental Health Administration, 1989.

The four-volume study on youth suicide commissioned by the Secretary of Health and Human Services.

Flaherty, Michael G. *An Assessment of the National Incidence of Juvenile Suicide in Adult Jails, Lockups, and Juvenile Detention Centers.* Washington, D.C.: Office of Juvenile Justice and Delinquency Prevention, 1980.

Patterns of juvenile suicide in criminal detention centers.

Frederick, Calvin J. *Self-Destructive Behavior Among Younger Age Groups.* Rockville, Md.: National Institute of Mental Health, 1976.

Examines patterns of self-destructive behavior in American youth.

Merry, James A. *Suicide Among Young People: A National Health Concern.* Atlanta: Centers for Disease Control, 1983.

Information on youth suicide.

National Institute of Mental Health. *Child and Adolescent Suicide.* Rockville, Md.: author, 1981.

A survey of literature on child and adolescent suicide.

Peters, Lori J. *Suicide: Theory, Identification, and Counseling Strategies.* Ann Arbor: University of Michigan, 1985.

Outlines suicide counseling strategies and describes warning signs of suicidal tendencies.

———*Teenage Suicide: Identification, Intervention and Prevention.* Ann Arbor: Educational Resources Information Center Counseling and Personnel Services Clearinghouse, 1985.

Guidelines for identifying and preventing potential teen suicides.

United States. Congress. House. Committee on Education and Labor. *Hearing on H.R. 457, the Youth Suicide Prevention Act: Hearing Before the Committee on Elementary, Secondary, and Vocational Education of the Committee on Education and Labor, House of Representatives.* 100th Cong. 1st sess., May 13, 1987. Washington, D.C.: U.S. Government Printing Office, 1987.

Probes proposed legislation on youth suicide prevention.

United States. Congress. House. Committee on Education and Labor. *Hearings on Youth Suicide Prevention Act of 1985: Hearings Before the Sub-*

committee on Youth Suicide Prevention Act of 1985: Hearings Before the Subcommittee on Elementary, Secondary, and Vocational Education of the Committee on Education and Labor, House of Representatives. 99th Cong., 1st sess., September 10 and October 21, 1985. Washington, D.C.: U.S. Government Printing Office, 1986.

Investigates aspects of proposed legislation on youth suicide prevention.

United States. Congress. House. Committee on Education and Labor. *Youth Suicide Prevention Act: Report Together with Supplemental Views (to accompany H.R. 4850).* Washington, D.C.: U.S. Government Printing Office, 1986.

Committee report on proposed youth suicide prevention legislation.

United States. Congress. House. Select Committee on Aging. Subcommittee on Human Services. *Suicide and Suicide Prevention: A Briefing.* Washington, D.C.: U.S. Government Printing Office, 1985.

Examines suicide among the elderly.

United States. Congress. *Joint Resolution to Authorize and Request the President to Designate the Month of June 1986 "Youth Suicide Prevention Month."* Washington, D.C.: U.S. Government Printing Office, 1986.

House and Senate resolution seeks presidential designation of Youth Suicide Prevention Month.

United States. Congress. Senate. Committee on the Judiciary. *Federal Role in Addressing the Tragedy of Youth Suicide: Hearing Before the Subcommittee on Juvenile Justice of the Committee on the Judiciary, United States Senate, on adequacy of current federal research and prevention efforts and the role of the Office of Juvenile Justice and Deliquency Prevention in Youth Suicides.* 99th Cong. 1st sess., Apr. 30, 1985. Washington, D.C.: U.S. Government Printing Office, 1985.

Reviews the federal government's research and prevention efforts in youth suicide.

United States. Congress. Senate. Committee on the Judiciary. *Teenage Suicide: Hearing Before the Subcommittee on Juvenile Justice of the Committee on the Judiciary, United States Senate.* 98th Cong. 2d sess., Oct. 3, 1984. Washington, D.C.: U.S. Government Printing Office, 1985.

Looks at factors that can lead to teenage suicide and prevention measures.

United States. Department of Health and Human Services. *Youth Suicide: Community Response to a National Tragedy*. Washington, D.C.: Department of Health and Human Services, 1985.

How communities have responded to the nationwide increase in youth suicide.

United States Navy Department. *Suicide Prevention Training Manual*. Washington, D.C.: author, 1986.

Training manual in suicide prevention prepared in association with the American Association of Suicidology.

Wadeson, Harriet. *Portraits of Suicide*. Rockville, Md.: National Institute of Mental Health, 1979.

Presents information on the mental and psychological profile of suicides.

BROCHURES AND PAMPHLETS

Allen, Nancy H., and Michael L. Peck. *Suicide in Young People*. West Point, Pa.: Merck Sharp and Dohme, n.d. 9p.

Outlines the causes of youth suicide, warning signs, and prevention measures. Includes bibliography.

Handbook of Living Will Laws, 1987 ed. New York: Society for the Right to Die, 1987.152p.

Comprehensive resource on the living will; includes information on legislation, court decisions, and other developments.

Lee, A. Russell, and Charlotte P. Ross. *Suicide in Youth and What You Can Do About It—A Guide for School Personnel*. West Point, Pa.: Merck Sharp and Dohme, n.d. 9p.

Provides background information, describes the potential victim, gives danger signs, and outlines preventive measures.

————*Suicide in Youth and What You Can Do About It - A Guide For Students*. West Point, Pa.: Merck Sharp and Dohme, n.d. 6p.

Designed to teach students how to recognize the warning signs and what to do when someone is contemplating suicide.

Right-to-Die Court Decisions. New York: Society for the Right to Die, n.d.

Two-volume set providing synopses of the major right-to-die court cases in the United States. Periodically updated.

Useful Information on . . . Suicide. Rockville, Md.: National Institute of Mental Health, 1986. 28p.

Pamphlet on suicide and suicide prevention prepared by the Public Health Service.

AUDIOVISUAL MATERIALS

And I'll Call You Tomorrow: Suicide. Trainex Corp, n.d. 25 min. Video.

People who have attempted suicide describe their feelings and recount the incidents that led to the attempt. Clues that someone may be considering suicide are explained.

Between. Colour Images Unlimited, 1977. 17 min. Video.

Avoiding statistics or medical terminology, portrays the problems of the suicidal through a series of sensitive images and sharp narration.

Childhood's End. Filmakers Library, 1981. 28 min. Video or 16 mm.

Examines the problem of adolescent suicide, the second leading cause of death in this age group.

Coping with Depression. Film Fair Communications, 1987. 30 min. Video.

Suicide prevention experts and teenagers who have confronted emotional depression outline survival techniques for young people.

Coping with Teen Suicide Series. The Center for Humanities, 1987. 30 min. Video. 2 programs.

Designed to help teens come to terms with the suicide of a classmate, friend, or family member and to recognize danger signs in themselves and others.

Deadline. Media Guild, 1986. 27 min. Video.

Examines some of the causes of and remedies for teenage suicide.

Dead Serious. MTI Film and Video, 1987. 24 min. Video or 16 mm.

Award-winning discussion of suicide warning signs, myths, and prevention measures. Based on the book by Jane Mersky Leder.

Depression and Suicide. The Cinema Guild, 1976. 26 min. Video.

Investigates some of the causes of depression among teenagers and explores ways to prevent feelings of loneliness from becoming overpowering and leading to self-destructive behavior.

Annotated Bibliography

Depression—Blahs, Blues, and Better Days. American Educational Films, 1973. 18 min. Video.

Explores the reasons behind the extensive substance abuse and high incidence of suicide among young adults. Discusses some suggested solutions.

A Dignified Exit. Filmakers Library, 1981. 26 min. Video.

Examines the ethics of suicide from the vantage points of a woman with cancer, an elderly woman with multiple sclerosis, and a woman whose husband died of cancer.

Don't Even. Brown Roa Publishing Media, 1989. 60 min. Video.

Opens with graphic scenes of a teen suicide victim and then explores the issue through personal stories.

Dying to Be Heard . . . Is Anybody Listening? Ivanhoe Communications, 1987. 25 min. Video.

Looks at the recent upsurge in teenage suicide and its causes.

Everything to Live For. MTI Teleprograms, 1982. 24 min. Video or 16 mm.

Four teenagers who have either attempted or succeeded at suicide are the subject of this case study.

Fragile Time. Perennial Education, n.d. 20 min. Video.

Profiles three suicidal teenagers and their families.

Hear Me Cry: Suicide Prevention. Coronet/MTI Film and Video, 1988. 30 min. Video.

CBS Schoolbreak Special that depicts the story of two teenage boys and their suicide pact.

"Help Me!" The Story of a Teenage Suicide. Phoenix/BFA Films, 1981. 25 min. Video.

Patterned on numbers of case histories, this fictional account traces the decisions and life crisis of a teenage girl that lead her to suicide's brink.

In Loveland: Study of a Teenage Suicide. MTI Teleprograms, 1982. 28 min. Video or 16 mm.

Examines the tragic string of events leading up to the suicide of a 15-year-old boy.

Suicide

The Inner Voice in Suicide. Psychological and Educational Films, 1986. 60 min. Video.

Shows a psychologist's interviews with a woman who attempted suicide to illustrate the pattern of self-hatred and hopelessness that often leads to suicide.

Is Anybody Listening? Brown Roa Publishing Media, 1989. 180 min. Video.

Six-part series examines problems facing teenagers today, including suicide and other self-destructive behaviors.

Is Anyone Listening: Teen-Age Suicide. Carousel Film and Video, 1984. 28 min. Video or 16 mm.

Experts offer observations on the precipitous upswing in teenage suicide in the past decade.

It Begins with You. University of Calgary Communications Media, 1987. 29 min. Video.

A case study of interactive suicide prevention, for professionals.

I Want to Die. Paulist Productions. Media Guild, n.d. 25 min. Video.

In this dramatization, a young man home from college tells his parents he intends to kill himself. Focuses on parent-teenager relationships.

A Last Cry for Help. Unicorn Video, 1979. 97 min. Video.

A seemingly ideal, beautiful high school student attempts suicide in this made-for-TV movie.

Last Cry for Help. Learning Corporation of America. Unicorn Video, 1980. 30 min. Video.

Addresses the attempted suicide of an alienated, depressed young girl. Shows her experiences prior to the attempt and her growing strength afterward as she learns to take control of her life.

The Number Ten Killer. Nebraska ETV Council for Higher Education, 1969. 30 min. Video.

Discusses statistical patterns and the psychological concepts relevant to suicide. Probes suicide causes and warning signals.

Point of Return. International Film Bureau, 1965. 24 min. Video.

A group of doctors, psychiatrists, and social workers refer to a case history to demonstrate misconceptions about the causes and related aspects of suicide.

Rational Suicide. Carousel Film and Video, 1981. 15 min. Video.

Explores whether rational suicide is a plausible option for people afflicted with pain and incurable disease.

Reach Out for Life. Filmakers Library, 1980. 11 min. Video.

Animated program dealing with one man's midlife crisis and contemplation of suicide.

Research in Family Life. RI Media Productions, 1974. 18 min. Video.

Addresses family life issues, including family medical problems, care of the elderly, and teen suicide.

The Right to Die . . . The Choice Is Yours. Society for the Right to Die, n.d. 14 min. Video with discussion guide.

Intended to educate viewers about their legal rights concerning the refusal of extraordinary life-saving measures. Explains the living will.

Ronnie's Tune. Wombat Productions, 1974. 18 min. Video.

Explores the sense of guilt and responsibility felt by those people a suicide victim leaves behind.

Rushes. Direct Cinema Limited, 1979. 56 min. Video.

A case study of suicide utilizing documentary techniques.

Scars. Women in Focus, 1987. 12 min. Video.

Probes the reasons behind and aftereffects of self-mutilation. Contains interviews with four women who slashed themselves.

Sometimes I Wonder If It's Worth It. Agency for Instructional Technology, 1985. 30 min. Video.

An analysis of teenage suicide intended to provoke discussion.

The Spirit Possession. Filmakers Library, 1981. 30 min. Video.

In this educational dramatization on suicide and the elderly, an 81-year-old Indian believes that evil spirits are driving him to take his own life.

Suicide. United Learning, 1986. 26 min. Video.

Designed to increase student awareness of suicide.

Suicide at 17. Lawren Production, n.d. Video or 16 mm.

A documentary on the self-destruction of a popular teenager outlining the facts of suicide and probing the causes and meanings.

Suicide

Suicide: A Teenage Crisis. CRM/McGraw-Hill Films, 1981. 110 min. Video.

A program examining the problem of teen suicide. Describes a variety of community and school initiatives to deal with the adolescent suicide crisis.

Suicide: But Jack Was a Good Driver. CRM/MacGraw-Hill Films, 1974. 15 min. Video.

A dramatization dealing with the high rate of suicide among young people.

Suicide Clinic: A Cry for Help. Indiana University Audio-Visual Center, 1969. 28 min. Video.

Looks at a suicide clinic where people are given a chance to talk out their problems.

Suicide: I Don't Want to Die. Cambridge Video, 1988. 30 min. Video or 16 mm, both with workbook.

Addresses when and how to approach someone who may be contemplating suicide.

Suicide Intervention. American Journal of Nursing, 1975. 30 min. Video.

Examines the nurse's potential to contribute to suicide intervention.

Suicide in the Elderly. McMaster University, 1980. 30 min. Video.

A primer on identifying and managing the problems of elderly patients with suicidal tendencies.

Suicide: It Doesn't Have to Happen. Phoenix/BFA Films, 1976. 21 min. Video.

Reviews many classic symptoms of teen suicide, based on actual case histories. Reflects on the reasons behind surges in adolescent suicide.

The Suicide Syndrome. Windsor Total Video, 1978. 30 min. Video.

A professor of psychiatry uses actual videotaped patient sessions to examine the behavioral patterns, problems, and methods of treatment specific to suicide patients.

Suicide: The Warning Signs. Centron Films, 1982. 24 min. Video.

A discussion of the common suicide warning signs and what steps family and friends should take when they occur.

Teen Suicide. ABC Community Relations, 1985. 22 min. Video.

Examines the problem of teenage suicide and its impact on family and friends. Reviews warning signs and suggests preventive actions.

Teenage Suicide. CBS News Magazine. MTI Teleprogram, 1979. 16 min. Video or 16 mm.

Sets out to account for the fact that suicide is the second leading cause of death among teenagers.

Teenage Suicide. Films, Inc., 1981. 60 min. Video.

Explores the emergent problem of teenage suicide.

Teenage Suicide: The Ultimate Dropout. PBS Video, 1979. 29 min. Video.

A 14-year-old girl describes how she actively considered suicide. The girl's mother recounts her own feelings.

Therapeutic Silence. American Journal of Nursing, 1982. 32 min. Video.

In this dramatization of an adolescent who is hospitalized after a suicide attempt, the young man becomes more responsive when a nurse includes him in activities that give him a chance to gain social support.

Top Secret: A Friend's Cry for Help. Human Relations Media, 1989. 30 min. Video.

Addresses the dilemma of promising not to reveal a friend's suicidal intentions.

What's a Parent to Do (Teenage Suicide). New Dimensions Media, 1986. 21 min. Video.

Looks at one community and school system and the measures they have taken to deal with teenage suicide.

Young People in Crisis. National Committee on Youth Suicide Prevention, 1989. 30 min. Video.

Through dramatic personal accounts, examines the problems adolescents face that lead them to attempt suicide. Explains effective means of intervention.

CHAPTER 7

―――――――――― ████ ――――――――――

ORGANIZATIONS AND ASSOCIATIONS

More than 1,000 suicide prevention centers, community mental health facilities, and crisis hot lines now exist across the United States. Their activities range from research, prevention, and education to counseling and outreach services. This chapter is a listing of organizations that are a source of information and educational materials on suicide. These organizations include government agencies, professional associations, foundations, and community facilities and groups. National organizations are accompanied by a brief synopsis of their involvement in suicide issues and the types of information they make available. Similar abstracts are not provided at the state and local level as the services and activities of these organizations are subject to frequent change.

NATIONAL ORGANIZATIONS

American Association of Suicidology
2459 S. Ash
Denver, CO 80222
(303) 692-0985
Professional association of individuals involved in suicide research and prevention. Operates national information clearinghouse. Publishes and distributes numerous materials on suicide.

American Medical Association
535 N. Dearborn Street
Chicago, IL 60610
(312) 645-5076
Major professional association of physicians. Maintains a special committee that studies suicide from a medical perspective. Provides information and materials on medicine and public health care.

American Psychiatric Association
1400 K Street N.W.
Washington, DC 20005
(202) 797-4900
Professional medical organization that provides an extensive range of materials on suicide.

American Psychological Association
1200 17 Street N.W.
Washington, DC 20036
(202) 833-7600
Professional medical organization that is a source of information and educational materials on psychological inquiry into self-destructive behavior.

American Suicide Foundation
1045 Park Avenue
New York, NY 10028
(212) 410-1111
Funds and supports suicide prevention through research and education.

Family Service Association of America
44 E. 23rd Street
New York, NY 10010
(212) 674-6100
Source of information on postvention, counseling, and outreach services for suicide survivors.

The Hemlock Society
PO Box 66218
Los Angeles, CA 90066
(213) 391-1871
Nonprofit educational organization that supports active voluntary euthanasia, or "self-deliverance." Source of information on legal and legislative developments.

National Center for Health Statistics
3700 East-West Highway
Hyattsville, MD 20782
(301) 436-8884
Collects, analyzes, and disseminates statistical data on the rate and incidence of suicide in the United States.

National Committee on Youth Suicide Prevention
825 Washington Street
Norwood, MA 02062
(617) 769-5686
Private network of professionals, officials, and individuals involved in efforts to reduce youth suicide. Source of a range of materials and information on the issue.

National Institute of Mental Health
5600 Fishers Lane
Rockville, MD 20857
(301) 443-3877
Part of the Public Health Service, the federal agency with primary responsibility for suicide research and prevention programs. Provides information and educational resources.

Samaritans
500 Commonwealth Avenue
Kenmore Square
Boston, MA 02215
(617) 247-0220
International lay order committed to befriending and helping the suicidal. Maintains walk-in services and crisis hot lines in local communities. Source of information on suicide and suicide prevention.

Society for the Right to Die
250 West 57th Street
New York, NY 10107
(212) 246-6973
Major national advocacy group for passive euthanasia and the right of the terminally ill to death with dignity. Prepares and disseminates materials on the living will, right-to-die court cases, and legislative and medical developments.

Youth Suicide National Center
445 Virginia Avenue
San Mateo, CA 94402
(213) 655-1974
Nonprofit organization that coordinates and supports youth suicide prevention activities. Serves as an information clearinghouse. Develops and distributes educational materials and other resources.

STATE AND LOCAL ORGANIZATIONS

ALABAMA

Contact Mobile
3224 Executive Park Circle
Mobile, AL 36606
(205) 473-5330

Crisis Center of East Alabama,
  Inc.
PO Box 1949
Auburn, AL 36830
(205) 821-8600

Crisis Center of Jefferson County
3600 8th Avenue S.
Birmingham, AL 35222
(205) 323-7782

Help A Crisis
101 Coliseum Boulevard
Montgomery, AL 36109
(205) 279-7830

Indian Rivers Mental Health
  Center
PO Box 2190
Tuscaloosa, AL 35403
(205) 345-1600

North Central Alabama Mental
  Health Center
PO Box 637
Decatur, AL 35601
(205) 355-6091

Riverbend Center for Mental
  Health
PO Box 941
Florence, AL 35630
(205) 764-3431

South Central Mental Health
  Board
PO Box 1028
Andalusia, AL 36420
(205) 222-2523

ALASKA

Central Peninsula Mental
  Health Center
11355 Kenai Spur Road,
  Suite 228
Kenai, AK 99611
(907) 283-7501

Fairbanks Crisis Clinic
  Foundation
PO Box 832
Fairbanks, AK 99707
(907) 479-0166

Gateway Mental Health
3134 Tongass
Ketchikan, AK 99901
(907) 225-4135

Juneau Mental Health Clinic
210 Admiral Way
Juneau, AK 99801
(907) 586-5280

Suicide Prevention and Crisis Center
2611 Fairbanks Street
Anchorage, AK 99503
(907) 272-2496

ARIZONA

Phoenix Crisis Intervention
  Program
1250 S. 7th Avenue
Phoenix, AZ 85007
(602) 258-8011

Safford Crisis Line
PO Box 956
Safford, AZ 85546
(602) 428-4550

Tucson Help On Call
Information and Referral Service
2555 E. First Street, Suite 107
Tucson, AZ 85716
(602) 323-1303

ARKANSAS

Contact Hot Springs
705 Malvern Avenue
Hot Springs, AR 71901
(501) 623-4048

Contact Pine Bluff
PO Box 8734
Pine Bluff, AR 71601
(501) 536-4228

Contact Little Rock
PO Box 2572
Little Rock, AR 72203
(501) 666-0235

Crisis Center of Arkansas, Inc.
1616 W. 14th Street
Little Rock, AR 72202
(501) 664-8834

CALIFORNIA

Contact Care Center
PO Box 901
Lafayette, CA 94549
(415) 284-2273

Contact Fresno
7172 N. Cedar
Fresno, CA 93710
(209) 298-8001

Contra Costa Crisis/Suicide
Intervention
PO Box 4852
Walnut Creek, CA 94596
(415) 939-1916

Crisis-Help of Napa Valley, Inc.
1360 Adams Street
St. Helena, CA 94574
(707) 942-4319

Crisis House/Crisis
Intervention Center
144 S. Orange
El Cajon, CA 92020
(714) 444-6506

Crisis Line Care Project
461 N. Franklin Street
Fort Bragg, CA 95437
(707) 964-4055

The Crisis Team
PO Box 85524
San Diego, CA 92138
(619) 236-4576

Lake County Mental Health
Emergency Services
922 Bevins Court
Lakeport, CA 95453
(707) 263-2258

Lifeline Community Services
200 Jefferson Street
Vista, CA 92083
(714) 726-6396

Los Angeles Suicide
Prevention Center
1041 S. Menlo
Los Angeles, CA 90006
(213) 386-5111

Marin Suicide Prevention
Center
PO Box 792
San Anselmo, CA 94960
(415) 454-4566

New Hope Counseling Center
12141 Lewis Street
Garden Grove, CA 92640
(714) 971-4123

North Bay Suicide
Prevention, Inc.
PO Box 2444
Napa, CA 94558
(707) 257-3470

Pasadena Mental Health
Center
1495 N. Lake
Pasadena, CA 91104
(213) 681-1381

San Francisco Suicide
Prevention
3940 Geary Boulevard
San Francisco, CA 94118
(415) 752-4866

San Joaquin County
Mental Health
1212 N. California
Stockton, CA 95202
(209) 948-1818

San Luis Obispo County
Hotline, Inc.
PO Box 654
San Luis Obispo, CA 93406
(805) 544-6164

171

Santa Barbara Crisis Intervention
Psychiatric Emergency Team
4444 Calle Real
Santa Barbara, CA 93110
(805) 964-6713

Santa Clara Suicide and
  Crisis Service
2220 Moorpark
San Jose, CA 95128
(408) 279-6250

Second Chance, Inc.
PO Box 643
Newark, CA 94560
(415) 792-4357

Sonoma Valley Family Center
  Crisis Intervention Program
PO Box 128
Sonoma, CA 95476
(707) 996-7877

Suicide and Crisis
  Intervention Service
1669 N. "E" Street
San Bernardino, CA 92405
(714) 886-6730

Suicide Prevention Center/
  Monterey County
PO Box 52078
Pacific Grove, CA 93950
(408) 375-6966

Suicide Prevention/Crisis
  Center of San Mateo County
1811 Trousdale Drive
Burlingame, CA 94010
(415) 877-5604

Suicide Prevention/Crisis
  Intervention of Alameda
  County
PO Box 9102
Berkeley, CA 94709
(415) 848-1515

Suicide Prevention of
  Yolo County
PO Box 622
Davis, CA 95617
(916) 756-7542

Suicide Prevention Service
  of Sacramento
PO Box 449
Sacramento, CA 95802
(916) 441-1138

Suicide Prevention Service
  of Santa Cruz County
PO Box 734
Capitola, CA 95010
(408) 426-2342

Sutter-Yuba Mental Health
  Crisis Clinic
1965 Live Oak Boulevard
Yuba City, CA 95991
(916) 674-8500

Valley Hotline
602 E. Florida
Hemet, CA 92343
(714) 658-7227

Ventura County Mental
  Health Department
300 Hillmont Avenue
Ventura, CA 93003
(805) 652-6727

COLORADO

Colorado Springs Crisis Services
Pikes Peak Mental Health
875 W. Moreno
Colorado Springs, CO 80903
(303) 417-3343

Comitis Crisis Center
9840 E. 17th Avenue
Aurora, CO 80040
(303) 341-9160

Crisis/Information Helpline
  of Larimer County
700 W. Mountain Avenue
Ft. Collins, CO 80521-2506
(303) 493-3896

Emergency Psychiatric Services
1333 Iris Avenue
Boulder, CO 80302
(303) 443-8500

Ft. Morgan Helpline
330 Meaker Street
Ft. Morgan, CO 80701
(303) 867-3411

Grand Junction Helpline
PO Box 3302
Grand Junction, CO 81502
(303) 245-3270

Pueblo Suicide Prevention, Inc.
229 Colorado Avenue
Pueblo, CO 81004
(303) 545-2477

Suicide and Crisis Control
2459 S. Ash
Denver, CO 80222
(303) 756-8485

CONNECTICUT

Contact of Southeast
  Connecticut, Inc.
PO Box 277
Uncasville, CT 06382
(203) 848-1655

Hotline of Greenwich, Inc.
189 Mason Street
Greenwich, CT 06830
(203) 661-4378

Info Line of Southwestern
  Connecticut
7 Academy Street
Norwalk, CT 06850
(203) 333-7555

Open Line, Ltd.
245 Post Road East
Westport, CT 06880
(203) 226-3546

The Wheeler Clinic, Inc.
91 Northwest Drive
Plainville, CT 06062
(203) 747-6801

DELAWARE

South New Castle County
  Community Mental Health
14 Central Avenue
New Castle, DE 19720
(302) 421-6711

Sussex County Community
  Mental Health Center
Georgetown, DE 19947
(302) 856-2151

DISTRICT OF COLUMBIA

D.C. Suicide Prevention
D.C. Department of Human
  Services
1905 E. Street S.E.
Washington, DC 20005
(202) 727-3622

St. Francis Center
2633 15th Street N.W., Suite 11
Washington, DC 20009
(202) 234-5613

FLORIDA

Alachua County Crisis Center
730 N. Waldo Road, Suite 100
Gainesville, FL 32601
(904) 372-3659

Brevard County Mental Health
  Center
566 Barton Boulevard, #304
Rockledge, FL 32955
(305) 631-9790

Columbia Counseling Center
PO Box 2818
Lake City, FL 32056
(904) 752-1045

Community Mental Health Center
Winter Haven Hospital
Winter Haven, FL 33880
(813) 293-1121

Contact Help Line
PO Box 2021
Lakeland, FL 33803
(813) 688-9114

Crisis Intervention Center of
  Broward County
PO Box 7537
Fort Lauderdale, FL 33338
(305) 763-1213

Crisis Intervention Services
Peace River Center
1745 Highway 17 S.
Bartow, FL 33830
(813) 533-3141

Crisis Line
205 Shell Avenue
Ft. Walton Beach, FL 32548
(904) 244-0151

Crisis Line Information and
  Referral Service
PO Box 15522
W. Palm Beach, FL 33416
(305) 689-3334

Ft. Myers Crisis Intervention
Center
Lee Mental Health Center
PO Box 06137
Ft. Myers, FL 33906
(813) 334-3537

Help Now in Osceola, Inc.
917 Emmett Street
Kissimmee, FL 32741
(305) 847-8811

Hotline/Information and Referral
PO Box 13087
St. Petersburg, FL 33733
(813) 536-9464

Manatee Mental Health Center
Crisis Services
PO Box 9478
Bradenton, FL 33506
(813) 747-8648

Mental Health Services of Orange
2520 N. Orange Avenue
Orlando, FL 32804
(305) 896-9306

Panama City Crisis Line
Northwest Mental Health Center
615 N. McArthur Avenue
Panama City, FL 32401
(904) 769-9481

Pensacola Help Line
Lakeview Center, Inc.
1221 W. Lakeview Street
Pensacola, FL 32501
(904) 432-1222

Suicide and Crisis Center
of Hillsborough County
2214 E. Henry Avenue
Tampa, FL 33610
(813) 238-8411

Suicide Prevention Service
2218 Park Street
Jacksonville, FL 32204
(904) 387-5641

Switchboard of Miami, Inc.
35 S.W. 8th Street
Miami, FL 33130
(305) 358-1640

GEORGIA

Cobb-Douglas Mental Health
Community Services Building
737 Church Street, Suite 420
Marietta, GA 30060
(404) 424-0870

Contact Chattahoochee Valley
PO Box 12002
Columbus, GA 31907
(404) 327-0199

Contact Hall County
PO Box 1616
Gainesville, GA 30503
(404) 536-7145

Crisis Line of Macon and
Bibb Counties
Mercer University
PO Box 56
Macon, GA 31207
(912) 745-9292

175

De Kalb Emergency/Crisis
  Intervention Service
Georgia Mental Health Institute
1256 Briarcliff Road N.E.
Atlanta, GA 30306
(404) 892-4646

Emergency Mental Health Service
99 Butler S.E.
Atlanta, GA 30311
(404) 522-9222

First Call for Help
PO Box 9119
Savannah, GA 31412
(912) 232-3383

Gwinnett County Mental Health
100 Clayton Street S.E.
Lawrenceville, GA 30245
(404) 963-8141

Help Line
PO Box 1724
Augusta, GA 30903
(404) 724-4357

HAWAII

Helpline Kauai
PO Box 3541
Lihue, HI 96766
(808) 822-7435

Helpline/Suicide and Crisis
  Center
95 Mahalani Street
Wailuku, HI 96793
(808) 244-7405

Kona Crisis Center, Inc.
PO Box 4363
Kailua-Kona, HI 96740
(808) 329-6744

Suicide and Crisis Center
200 N. Vineyard Boulevard,
  Room 603
Honolulu, HI 96817
(808) 536-7234

IDAHO

Kellog Emergency Line
Health and Welfare Service
  Center
313 W. Cameron
Kellog, ID 83837
(208) 784-1351

Region IV Services/Mental Health
1105 S. Orchard
Boise, ID 83705
(208) 338-7020

Twin Falls Emergency Services
Region 5 Mental Health
823 Harrison
Twin Falls, ID 83301
(208) 734-9770

W. George Moody Health Center
2195 Ironwood Court
Coeur d'Alene, ID 83814
(208) 667-6406

YWCA Crisis Services
300 Main Street
Lewiston, ID 83501
(208) 746-9655

ILLINOIS

Cairo Crisis Line
Mental Health Center
218 10th Street
Cairo, IL 62914
(618) 734-2665

Chicago Crisis Intervention
City of Chicago Department
  of Human Services
640 N. La Salle
Chicago, IL 60610
(312) 744-4045

Christian County Mental Health
  Center
301 S. Webster
Taylorville, IL 62568
(217) 824-4905

Community Counseling Services
1315 Vandalia
Collingsville, IL 62234
(618) 344-0393

Community Crisis Center
PO Box 1390
Elgin, IL 60121
(312) 742-4031

Contact Danville
504 N. Vermilion
Danville, IL 61832
(217) 446-8212

Contact Rockford
PO Box 1976
Rockford, IL 61110
(815) 964-0400

Crisis Line of Will County
PO Box 2354
Joliet, IL 60435
(815) 744-5280

Crisis Services of Madison
  County
PO Box 570
Wood River, IL 62095
(618) 251-4073

Dewitt County Human
  Resource Center
109 W. Jefferson
Clinton, IL 61727
(217) 935-9496

Highland Community
  Counseling Services
508 Broadway
Highland, IL 62249
(618) 654-7232

Lincoln Crisis Clinic
A. Lincoln Mental Health Center
315 8th
Lincoln, IL 62656
(217) 732-2161

Madison County Mental Health
  Center
1625 Edwards Street
Alton, IL 62002
(618) 462-3505

Mental Health Center
2024 State Street
Granite City, IL 62040
(618) 877-4420

Montgomery County Counseling
  Services
200 S. Main Street
Hillsboro, IL 62049
(217) 532-9581

Mt. Vernon Crisis Line
601 N. 18th
PO Box 428
Mt. Vernon, IL 62864
(618) 242-1510

Peoria Call For Help
5407 N. University
Peoria, IL 61614
(309) 692-1766

Quincy Suicide Prevention and
  Crisis Service
4409 Maine
Quincy, IL 62301
(217) 223-0413

Society of Samaritans-Chicago
5638 S. Woodlawn Avenue
Chicago, IL 60637
(312) 947-8844

Spoon River Community Mental
  Health Center
302 E. Main Street, Suite 530
Galesburg, IL 61401
(309) 343-5155

Suicide and Crisis Intervention
  Service
500 Wilshire Drive
Belleville, IL 62223
(618) 397-0968

Sullivan Crisis Line
Moultree County Counseling
  Center
2 W. Adams
Sullivan, IL 61951
(217) 728-4358

Union County Counseling Service
204 South Street
Anna, IL 62906
(618) 833-8551

INDIANA

Contact-Cares of NW Indiana
PO Box 8143
Merrillville, IN 46410
(219) 769-3278

Contact Putnam County
PO Box 15
Greencastle, IN 46135
(317) 653-5040

Lafayette Crisis Center
803 N. 8th Street
Lafayette, IN 47904
(317) 742-0244

Lawrenceburg Crisis Line
Community Mental Health Center
285 Bielby Road
Lawrenceburg, IN 47025
(812) 537-1302

Mental Health Association in
  Marion County
1433 N. Meridian Street,
  Room 202
Indianapolis, IN 46202
(317) 269-1569

Southwestern Indiana
  Mental Health Center
415 Mulberry
Evansville, IN 47713
(812) 423-7791

Twin Lakes Contact-Help
PO Box 67
Monticello, IN 47960
(219) 583-4357

IOWA

Aid Center
406 5th Street
Sioux City, IA 51101
(712) 252-1861

Foundation 2, Inc.
1251 Third Avenue S.E.
Cedar Rapids, IA 52403
(319) 362-2176

Integrated Crisis Service
2530 University Avenue
Waterloo, IA 50701
(319) 233-8484

Iowa City Crisis Intervention
  Center
26 E. Market
Iowa City, IA 52240
(319) 351-2726

Suicide Help-Line of Iowa
PO Box 711
Clearlake, IA 50428
(515) 357-4357

KANSAS

Area Mental Health Center
W. Highland 50 Bypass
Dodge City, KS 67801
(316) 227-8566

Garden City Area Mental Health
  Center
156 Gardendale
Garden City, KS 67846
(316) 276-7689

Hotline Crisis Information
and Referral
PO Box 1982
Salina, KS 67402-1878
(913) 827-4803

Sedgwick County Department
of Mental Health
1801 E. Tenth Street
Wichita, KS 67214-3197
(316) 268-8251

Mental Health Center of
East-Central Kansas
705 S. Commercial
Emporia, KS 66801
(316) 342-6116

Shawnee Community Mental
Health Center
2401 W. 6th
Topeka, KS 66606
(913) 233-1370

Regional Crisis Center
PO Box 164
Manhattan, KS 66502
(913) 539-2785

Wyandotte Mental Health Center
36th and Eaton
Kansas City, KS 66103
(913) 831-9500

Ulysses Area Mental Health Center
102 W. Flower
Ulysses, KS 76880
(316) 356-3198

KENTUCKY

Barren River Mental Health
822 Woodway Drive
Bowling Green, KY 42101
(502) 843-4382

Cumberland River Comprehensive
Care Center
American Greeting Road
PO Box 568
Corbin, KY 40701
(606) 528-7010

Cave Run Comprehensive Care
Center
325 E. Main Street
Morehead, KY 40351
(606) 784-4161

Green River Comprehensive Care
Center
1001 Fredericka Street
Owensboro, KY 42301
(502) 683-0277

Crisis Intervention Mental Health
201 Mechanic Street
Lexington, KY 40507
(606) 254-3844

Kentucky River Community Care
PO Box 603
Jackson, KY 41339
(606) 666-4904

Landsdowne Mental Health Center
PO Box 790
Ashland, KY 41101
(606) 324-1141

N. Central Comprehensive Care
  Center
907 N. Dixie Avenue
Elizabethtown, KY 42701
(502) 769-1304

Northern Kentucky
  Comprehensive Care Center
503 Farrell Drive
Covington, KY 41012
(606) 331-6505

Pennyroyal Regional Mental Health
735 N. Drive
Hopkinsville, KY 42240
(502) 886-5163

Seven Counties Services
Crisis and Information Center
600 S. Preston Street
Louisville, KY 40202
(502) 583-3951

Somerset Emergency Services
Community Mental Health
  Services
324 Cundiff Square
Somerset, KY 42501
(606) 679-7348

LOUISIANA

Baton Rouge Crisis Intervention
  Center
PO Box 80738
Baton Rouge, LA 70898
(504) 924-1595

Mental Health Association
  of New Orleans
Crisis Line Program
2515 Canal Street, Suite 200
New Orleans, LA 70199
(504) 821-1024

River Oaks Crisis Center
1525 River Oaks Road W.
New Orleans, LA 70123
(504) 734-1740

SW Louisiana Education
  and Referral Center
PO Box 3844
Lafayette, LA 70502
(318) 232-4357

MAINE

Crisis Stabilization Unit
147 Water Street
Skowhegan, ME 04976
(207) 474-2506

Dial Help
43 Illinois Avenue
Bangor, ME 04401
(207) 947-6143

Ingraham Volunteers, Inc.
142 High Street
Portland, ME 04101
(207) 773-4830

Suicide

MARYLAND

Baltimore Crisis Center
Walter P. Carter Mental
  Health Center
630 W. Fayette Street
Baltimore, MD 21201
(301) 528-2200

Contact Baltimore
710 N. Charles Street
Baltimore, MD 21201
(301) 332-0567

Montgomery County Hotline
10920 Connecticut Avenue
Kensington, MD 20795
(301) 949-1255

MASSACHUSETTS

Contact Boston
PO Box 287
Newtonville, MA 02160
(617) 244-4353

Greater Lawrence Mental
  Health Center
351 Essex Street
Lawrence, MA 01840
(617) 683-6303

Northampton Emergency Services
48 Pleasant Street
Northampton, MA 01060
(413) 586-5555

Psychiatric Associates of
  Lawrence
42 Franklin Street
Lawrence, MA 01840
(617) 682-7442

The Samaritans
500 Commonwealth Avenue
Boston, MA 02215
(617) 536-2460

Samaritans of Fall River-
  New Bedford, Inc.
386 Stanley Street
Fall River, MA 02720
(617) 636-1111

Samaritans of Merrimack Valley
55 Jackson Street
Lawrence, MA 01840
(617) 688-6607

Samaritans of Salem
PO Box 8133
Salem, MA 01970
(617) 744-5000

Samaritans of South
  Middlesex, Inc.
73 Union Avenue
Framingham, MA 01701
(617) 875-4500

Samaritans on Cape Cod
PO Box 65
Falmouth, MA 02540
(617) 548-8900

Valley Human Services
96 South Street
Ware, MA 01082
(413) 967-6241

MICHIGAN

Center for Human Resources
1113 Military Street
Port Huron, MI 48060
(313) 985-5168

Community Mental Health
Services of Muskegon County
125 E. Southern
Muskegon, MI 49442
(616) 726-5266

Genesse County Mental Health
420 W. 5th Avenue
Flint, MI 48503
(313) 257-3742

Lapeer County Community
Mental Health Center
1575 Suncrest Drive
Lapeer, MI 48446
(313) 667-0500

Macomb County Crisis Center
5th Floor, County Building
Mt. Clemens, MI 48043
(313) 578-8700

Oceana County Community
Mental Health
PO Box 127
Hart, MI 49420
(616) 873-2108

Ottawa County Mental
Health Center
1111 Fulton Street
Grand Haven, MI 49417
(616) 873-2108

Riverwood Community
Mental Health Center
Memorial Hospital
2681 Morton Avenue
St. Joseph, MI 49085
(616) 983-7781

St. Clair County Community
Mental Health Services
3415 28th Street
Port Huron, MI 48060
(313) 985-9618

Suicide Prevention Center/Detroit
220 Bagley, Suite 626
Detroit, MI 48226
(313) 963-7890

Washtenaw County Community Mental Health Center
2929 Plymouth Road
Ann Arbor, MI 48105
(313) 994-2285

Suicide

MINNESOTA

Contact Twin Cities
83 S. 12th Street
Minneapolis, MN 55403
(612) 341-2212

Hennepin County Medical
  Center
701 Park Avenue S.
Minneapolis, MN 55415
(612) 347-3164

Listening Ear Crisis Center
111 17th Avenue E.
Alexandria, MN 56308
(612) 762-1511

Owatonna-Steele County Contact
PO Box 524
Owatonna, MN 55060
(507) 451-1897

Southwestern Mental Health
  Center
1224 Fourth Avenue
Worthington, MN 56187
(507) 372-7671

Victims Crisis Center
908 N.W. 1st Drive
Austin, MN 55912
(507) 437-6680

MISSISSIPPI

Contact Jackson
PO Box 5192
Jackson, MS 39216
(601) 969-2077

Golden Triangle Contact
PO Box 1304
Columbus, MS 39703-1304
(601) 328-0200

Weems Mental Health Center
PO Box 4378
1415 College Road
Meridian, MS 39301
(601) 483-4821

MISSOURI

Contact St. Louis
PO Box 160070
St. Louis, MO 36116
(314) 771-0404

Joplin Crisis Intervention
PO Box 582
Joplin, MO 64801
(417) 781-2255

Kansas City Suicide
  Prevention Line
Western Missouri Mental
  Health Center
66 E. 22nd Street
Kansas City, MO 64108
(816) 471-3000

St. Joseph Crisis Service
St. Joseph State Hospital
St. Joseph, MO 64506
(816) 232-8431

MONTANA

Great Falls Crisis Center
PO Box 124
Great Falls, MT 59403
(406) 453-6512

Missoula Crisis Center, Inc.
PO Box 9345
Missoula, MT 59807
(406) 543-4555

Southwest Montana Mental
  Health Center
572 Logan
Helene, MT 59601
(406) 443-9667

Yellowstone County Welfare
3021 3rd Ave. N.
Billings, MT 59191
(406) 248-1691

NEBRASKA

Great Plains Mental Health
  Center
PO Box 1209
North Platte, NE 69103
(308) 532-4050

Northern Nebraska Mental
  Health Center
201 Miller Avenue
Norfolk, NE 68701
(402) 371-7530

Omaha Personal Crisis
  Service, Inc.
4102 Woolworth Avenue
Omaha, NE 68105
(402) 444-7335

Personal Crisis Service
PO Box 80083
Lincoln, NE 68506
(402) 475-5171

NEVADA

Las Vegas Suicide Prevention
  Center
2408 Santa Clara Drive
Las Vegas, NV 89104
(702) 732-1622

Suicide Prevention and Crisis
  Call Center
PO Box 8016
Reno, NV 89507
(702) 323-4533

NEW HAMPSHIRE

Center for Life Management
Salem Professional Park
44 Stiles Road
Salem, NH 03079
(603) 893-3548

Counseling Center of
  Sullivan County
18 Bailey Avenue
Claremont, NH 03743
(603) 542-2578

Emergency Services/Concord
PO Box 2032
Concord, NH 03301
(603) 228-1551

The Samaritans of Keene
25 Lamson Street
Keene, NH 03431
(603) 357-5505

Greater Manchester Mental
  Health Center
401 Cypress Street
Manchester, NH 03103
(603) 668-4111

Seacoast Mental Health Center
1145 Sagamore Avenue
Portsmouth, NH 03801
(603) 431-6703

Strafford Guidance Center, Inc.
180 Washington Street
Dover, NH 03820
(603) 742-0630

NEW JERSEY

Atlantic City Medical Center
1925 Pacific Avenue
Atlantic City, NJ 08401
(609) 344-1118

Contact of Mercer County
310 Sullivan Way
W. Trenton, NJ 08628
(609) 883-2880

Contact Atlantic City
PO Box 181
Linwood, NJ 08221
(609) 646-2101

Contact Morris-Passaic
PO Box 219
Pequannock, NJ 07440
(201) 831-1870

Contact Burlington County
PO Box 333
Moorestown, NJ 08057
(609) 234-5484

Contact of Ocean County
PO Box 1121
Toms River, NJ 08753
(201) 240-6104

Contact Gloucester County
PO Box 222
Richwood, NJ 08074
(609) 881-6200

Contact Union-Essex
PO Box 225
Roselle, NJ 07203
(201) 241-9350

Contact Help of Salem County
PO Box 36
Salem, NJ 08079
(609) 935-4484

Contact-We Care
PO Box 37
Westfield, NJ 07090
(201) 232-2936

Cumberland County
  Guidance Center
RD 1, Carmel Road
PO Box 808
Millville, NJ 08332
(609) 825-6810

Greater Manchester Mental
  Health Center
401 Cypress Street
Manchester, NJ 03103
(603) 688-4111

Guidance Center of Camden
  County
1660 Haddon Avenue
Camden, NJ 08103
(609) 428-1300

Guideline
500 N. Bridge
Bridgewater, NJ 08807
(201) 725-2800

Hunterdon Helpline
Route 31, Box 36
Flemington, NJ 08822
(201) 782-4357

Memo Hotline
100 Madison Avenue
Morristown, NJ 07960
(201) 540-5168

Newark Emergency Services
Mt. Carmel Guild Community
  Mental Health Center
17 Mulberry Street
Newark, NJ 07102
(201) 596-4100

North Essex Help Line
Mental Health Resource Center
60 S. Fullerton Avenue
Montclair, NJ 07042
(201) 744-6522

South Bergen Mental Health
  Center
395 Main Street
Hackensack, NJ 07601
(609) 460-0160

NEW MEXICO

Agora
The University of New Mexico
  Crisis Center
Student Union
PO Box 29
Albuquerque, NM 87131
(505) 277-3013

Bernalillo County Medical
  Health Center
2600 Maple N.E.
Albuquerque, NM 87106
(505) 843-2800

Suicide

NEW YORK

Androscoggin Valley
  Mental Health Clinic
Pageville Road
Berlin, NY 03570
(603) 752-7404

Buffalo Suicide Prevention
  and Crisis Service
3258 Main Street
Buffalo, NY 14214
(716) 834-3131

Contact Monmouth County
PO Box 137
Lincroft, NY 07738
(201) 544-1444

Contact Syracuse
958 Salt Springs Road
Syracuse, NY 13224
(315) 446-2610

Family of New Paltz
2 Church Street
New Paltz, NY 12561
(914) 255-8801

Family of Woodstock
16 Rock City Road
Woodstock, NY 12498
(914) 338-2370

Islip Hotline
Town Hall
Islip, NY 11751
(516) 277-4700

Jamestown Crisis Line
Jamestown General Hospital
Jamestown, NY 14701
(716) 484-1161, x321

Life Line/Health Association
  of Rochester
973 East Avenue
Rochester, NY 14607
(716) 271-3540

Niagara Hotline Crisis
  Intervention Service
775 3rd Street
Niagara Falls, NY 14302
(716) 285-9636

Orange County Help Line
Mental Health Association
255 Greenwich Avenue
Goshen, NY 10924
(914) 294-7411

Peekskill Crisis Intervention
1137 Main Street
Peekskill, NY 10566
(914) 739-6403

Plattsburgh Community
  Crisis Center
29 Protection Avenue
Plattsburgh, NY 12901
(518) 561-2331

Response of Suffolk
  County, Inc.
PO Box 300
Stony Brook, NY 11790
(516) 751-7620

Samaritans of Capital District
200 Central Avenue
Albany, NY 12206
(518) 463-0861

Suicide Prevention and
  Crisis Service
PO Box 312
Ithaca, NY 14950
(607) 272-1505

Utica Crisis Intervention
1213 Court Street, Cottage 46
Utica, NY 13502
(315) 797-6800, x4210

Westchester County Medical
  Center
Grasslands Road
Valhalla, NY 10595
(914) 347-7075

NORTH CAROLINA

Chapel Hill Helpline
33 McMasters Street
Chapel Hill, NC 27514
(919) 929-0479

Contact: Winston-Salem
1111 W. First Street
Winston-Salem, NC 27101
(919) 723-4338

Contact-Asheville/Buncombe
PO Box 6747
Ashville, NC 28816
(704) 252-7703

Council of Fayetteville, Inc.
PO Box 456
Fayetteville, NC 28302
(919) 483-8970

Contact Durham
806 A Clarendom Street
Durham, NC 27705
(919) 683-2392

Halifax County Mental Health
PO Box 1199
Roanoke Rapids, NC 27870
(919) 537-2909

Contact High Point
462 S. Main Street
High Point, NC 27260
(919) 885-0191

Helpline of Morehead
PO Box 3537
Morehead, NC 28557
(919) 755-6555

Contact Johnston County
140 Market Street
Smithfield, NC 27577
(919) 934-6979

Lee County Mental Health
  Crisis Line
130 Carbonton Road
Sanford, NC 27330
(919) 744-6521

Contact Lexington
PO Box 924
Lexington, NC 27292
(704) 249-8824

Human Services Center
Wiccacon Center
PO Box 407
Harrellsville, NC 27942
(919) 356-2938

Suicide and Crisis Service
  Alamance County
PO Box 2573
Burlington, NC 27215
(919) 228-1720

Wayne County Mental
  Health Center
301 N. Herman Street
Goldsboro, NC 27514
(919) 736-7330

Wilson Crisis Center
PO Box 593
Wilson, NC 27893
(919) 237-5156

NORTH DAKOTA

Fargo Hotline
PO Box 447
Fargo, ND 58107
(701) 293-6462

Grand Forks Mental Health
  Crisis Line
1407 24th Avenue S.
Grand Forks, ND 58201
(701) 746-9411

Minot Suicide Prevention Service
St. Josephs Hospital
Minot, ND 58701
(701) 857-2000

West Central Human Service
  Center
600 S. 2nd Street
Bismark, ND 58501
(701) 255-3090

OHIO

Contact Ashtabula
PO Box 674
Ashtabula, OH 44004
(216) 998-2609

Contact Crawford County
PO Box 631
Bucyrus, OH 44820
(419) 562-9009

Contact Queen City
PO Box 42071
Cincinnati, OH 45242
(513) 791-5673

Crisis Intervention Center
  of Stark County
2421 13th Street, N.W.
Canton, OH 44708
(216) 452-9812

Drake County Medical Health
  Clinic
212 E. Main
Greenville, OH 45331
(513) 548-1635

Greene County Crisis Center
452 W. Market
Xenia, OH 45385
(513) 376-8700

Information and Crisis Service/
Fairfield County
PO Box 1054
Lancaster, OH 43130
(614) 687-0500

Marysville Crisis Hotline
Charles B. Mills Center
715 Plum Street
Marysville, OH 43040
(614) 943-2916

Oxford Crisis and Referral
Center
111 E. Walnut Street
Oxford, OH 45056
(513) 523-4146

Preble Counseling Center
Hotline
101 North Barron Street
Eaton, OH 45320
(513) 456-1166

Scioto-Paint Valley Mental
Health Center
425 Chestnut Street
Chillicothe, OH 45601
(614) 773-0760

Shelby Helpline
60½ W. Main Street
Shelby, OH 44875
(419) 347-6307

Six County Crisis Hotline
2845 Bell Street
Zanesville, OH 43701
(614) 454-9766

Suicide Prevention Center,
Inc.
184 Salem Avenue
Dayton, OH 45406
(513) 223-9096

Suicide Prevention Center
Life-Line
1101 East High Street
Springfield, OH 45505
(513) 328-5300

Suicide Prevention Services
1301 High
Columbus, OH 43201
(614) 299-6600

Toledo First Call for Help
1 Stranahan Square, #141
Toledo, OH 43604
(419) 244-3728

OKLAHOMA

Contact Northwest Oklahoma
PO Box 3165
Enid, OK 73702
(405) 237-8400

Contact of Metropolitan
Oklahoma City
PO Box 12832
Oklahoma City, OK 73157
(405) 840-9396

Contact Western Oklahoma
PO Box 572
Clinton, OK 73601
(405) 323-1064

Helpline/Ponca City
PO Box 375
Ponca City, OK 74602
(405) 765-5551

Tulsa Helpline
PO Box 52847
Tulsa, OK 74152
(918) 585-1144

United Way Helpline
319 W. Main Street
Norman, OK 73069
(405) 364-3800

OREGON

Benton County Mental Health
530 N.W. 27th
Corvallis, OR 97401
(503) 757-6846

Linn County Mental Health
PO Box 100
Albany, OR 97321
(503) 967-3866

Josephine County Information
  and Referral Service
PO Box 670
Grants Pass, OR 97526
(503) 479-2349

Mental Health Emergency Center
151 W. 5th Street
Eugene, OR 97401
(503) 687-3608

Metro Crisis Intervention Service
PO Box 637
Portland, OR 97207
(503) 226-3099

PENNSYLVANIA

Contact Altoona
PO Box 11
Altoona, PA 16603
(814) 946-0531

Contact Lancaster
447 E. King Street
Lancaster, PA 17602
(717) 291-2261

Contact Beaver Valley
PO Box 75
New Brighton, PA 15066
(412) 728-3650

Contact Lower Bucks
PO Box 376
Newtown, PA
(215) 860-1803

Contact Chambersburg
221 N. Main Street
Chambersburg, PA 17201
(717) 263-8007

Contact Penn-Ohio
PO Box 91
Sharpsville, PA 16150
(412) 962-5777

Contact Harrisburg
PO Box 6270
Harrisburg, PA 17112
(717) 652-4987

Contact Philadelphia
PO Box 12586
Philadelphia, PA 19151
(215) 877-9099

Contact York
145 S. Duke Street
York, PA 17403
(717) 845-9125

Delaware County Crisis
  Intervention
600 N. Olive Street
Media, PA 19063
(215) 565-2041

Hazelton-Nanticoke Mental
  Health Center
W. Washington Street
Nanticoke, PA 18634
(717) 735-7590

Helpline/Pittsburgh
200 Ross Street
Pittsburgh, PA 15219
(412) 255-1133

Lehigh Valley Lifeline-Valley
  Wide Help
1244 Hamilton St
Allentown, PA 18102
(215) 435-7111

Perry County Human Services
Courthouse Annex
New Bloomfield, PA 17068
(717) 582-8052

Philadelphia Suicide and
  Crisis Intervention Center
1101 Market, 7th floor
Philadelphia, PA 19107
(215) 686-4420

United Way of Erie County
110 W. 10th Street
Erie, PA 16501-1466
(814) 453-5656

Williamsport Helpline
815 S. 4th Street
Williamsport, PA 17701
(717) 323-8555

RHODE ISLAND

The Samaritans of Providence
33 Chestnut Street
Providence, RI 02903
(401) 272-4044

Sympatico
29 Columbia Street
Wakefield, RI 02879
(401) 783-0650

SOUTH CAROLINA

Aiken County Crisis Line
PO Box 2712
Aiken, SC 29801
(803) 648-9900

Help-Line/Greenville
PO Box 1085
Greenville, SC 29602
(803) 233-HELP

Helpline of Midland, Inc.
PO Box 6336
Columbia, SC 29260
(803) 771-4357

SOUTH DAKOTA

Community Crisis Line
313 S. 1st Avenue
Sioux Falls, SD 57102
(605) 334-7022

New Beginnings Center
1206 North Third
Aberdeen, SD 57401
(605) 229-1239

TENNESSEE

Contact-Concern
PO Box 798
Kingsport, TN 37662
(615) 246-2273

Contact of Oak Ridge
PO Box 641
Oak Ridge, TN 37830
(615) 482-4949

Contact Ministries
PO Box 1403
Johnson City, TN 37601
(615) 926-0144

Contact Telephone of Knoxville
PO Box 11234
Knoxville, TN 37933-1234
(615) 523-9124

Contact of Blount County
PO Box 0382
Maryville, TN 37803
(615) 984-7689

Crisis Intervention Center, Inc.
PO Box 120934
Nashville, TN 37212
(615) 244-7444

Contact of Chattanooga
1202 Duncan
Chattanooga, TN 37404
(615) 266-8228

Helen Ross McNabb Center
1520 Cherokee Trail
Knoxville, TN 37920
(615) 637-9711

Contact of Cleveland
PO Box 962
Cleveland, TN 37311
(615) 479-9666

Suicide/Crisis Intervention
  Service/Memphis
PO Box 40068
Memphis, TN 38104
(901) 274-7477

Tullahoma Contact-Life Line
PO Box 1614
Tullahoma, TN 37388
Coffee County: (615) 455-7133
Franklin County: (615) 967-7133
Bedford County: (615) 684-7133
Moore County: (615) 759-7133

TEXAS

Concho Valley Center for
  Human Advance
244 N. Magdalen
San Antonio, TX 76903
(915) 653-5933

Contact Lubbock
PO Box 6377
Lubbock, TX 79493-6477
(806) 765-8393

Contact San Antonio
PO Box 5217
San Antonio, TX 78201
(512) 736-1876

Contact Tarrant County
PO Box 1431
Arlington, TX 76010
(817) 277-2233

Crisis Intervention of Houston,
  Inc.
PO Box 13066
Houston, TX 77219
Central: (713) 228-1505
Bay Area: (713) 333-5111

Crisis Services/Corpus Christi
4906-B Everhart
Corpus Christi, TX 78411
(512) 993-7410

Edinburgh Help Line
PO Box 1108
Edinburgh, TX 78539
(512) 383-0121

El Paso Crisis Intervention
  Services
5308 El Paso Drive
El Paso, TX 79905
(915) 779-1800

Information Hotline &
  Crisis Center
102 Neches
Austin, TX 78705
(512) 472-HELP

Plano Crisis Center
PO Box 1808
Plano, TX 75074
(214) 881-0088

Richardson Crisis Center
PO Box 877
Richardson, TX 75080
(214) 783-0008

Suicide & Crisis Center
2808 Swiss Avenue
Dallas, TX 75204
(214) 828-1000

Suicide Prevention/Crisis Center
PO Box 3250
Amarillo, TX 79106
(806) 376-4251

Suicide Rescue, Inc.
2750 I-10E
Beaumont, TX 77703
(713) 833-2311

Tarrant County Crisis Intervention
716 Magnolia
Ft. Worth, TX 76104
(817) 336-3355

UTAH

Salt Lake City Crisis Intervention
50 N. Medical Drive
Salt Lake City, UT 84132
(801) 581-2296

Salt Lake County Division of
  Mental Health
6856 South 700 East
Midvale, UT 84047
(801) 566-2455

Salt Lake County Division of
  Mental Health
54 South 700 East
Salt Lake City, UT 84102
(801) 531-8909

Weber County Mental Health
  Center
2510 Washington Boulevard,
  5th floor
Ogden, UT 84401
(801) 626-9100

VERMONT

Hotline for Help, Inc.
17 Elliot Street
Brattleboro, VT 05301
(802) 257-7989

Orange County Mental
  Health Service
PO Box G
Randolph, VT 05060
(802) 728-9641

St. Albans Emergency & Crisis Service
8 Ferris Street
St. Albans, VT 05478
(802) 524-6554

VIRGINIA

Alexandria Community
  Mental Health Center
206 N. Washington Street,
  5th floor
Alexandria, VA 22314
(703) 836-5751

Bristol Crisis Center
PO Box 642
Bristol, VA 24203-0642
(703) 466-2312

Contact Martinsville-Henry
  County
PO Box 1287
Martinsville, VA 24112
(703) 632-7295

Contact Peninsula
211 32nd Street
Newport News, VA 23607
(804) 245-0041

Contact Tidewater
PO Box 23
Virginia Beach, VA 23458
(804) 428-2211

Contact Tri-City Area
PO Box 942
Petersburg, VA 23803
(804) 733-1100

Crisis Line of Central Virginia
PO Box 2376
Lynchburg, VA 24501
(804) 528-HELP

Danville Helpline
382 Taylor Drive
Danville, VA 24541
Danville: (804) 799-1414
Chatham: (804) 432-0639
Gretna: (804) 656-1231

Fredericksburg Hotline
PO Box 7132
Fredericksburg, VA 22404
(703) 321-1212

Richmond County Mental
   Health Center
501 N. 9th Street, Room
   205
Richmond, VA 23218
(804) 780-8003

Roanoke Valley Trouble Center
360 Washington Avenue
Roanoke, VA 24016
(703) 563-0311

Suicide-Crisis Center, Inc.
PO Box 1493
Portsmouth, VA 23705
(804) 399-6393

WASHINGTON

Bremerton Crisis Clinic
500 Union
Bremerton, WA 98312
(206) 479-3033

Central Washington
   Comprehensive Mental
   Health
PO Box 959
Yakima, WA 98907
(509) 575-4200

Contact Tri-Cities Area
PO Box 684
Richland, WA 99352
(509) 943-6606

Crisis Clinic
1530 Eastlake East
Seattle, WA 98102
(206) 447-3222

Crisis Clinic/Thurston
   and Macon County
PO Box 2463
Olympia, WA 98507
(206) 352-2211

Ellensburg Crisis Line
507 Nanum
Ellensburg, WA 98926
(509) 925-4168

Suicide

Grant County Crisis Line
Mental Health and Family
  Service
PO Box 1057
Moses Lake, WA 98837
(509) 765-1717

Lewis County Information
  and Referral/Hotline
PO Box 337
Chehalis, WA 98532
(206) 748-6601

Spokane City Community
  Mental Health
S. 107 Division
Spokane, WA 99202
(509) 838-4428

Tacoma Crisis Clinic
PO Box 5007
Tacoma, WA 98405
(206) 759-6700

Whatcom County Crisis Services
124 E. Holly Street, #201
Bellingham, WA 98225
(206) 734-7271

Whitman County Crisis Line
PO Box 2615
Pullman, WA 99163
(509) 332-1505

WEST VIRGINIA

Contact-Care of Southern
  West Virginia
PO Box 581
Oak Hill, WV 25901
(304) 877-3535

Contact Huntington
520 11th Street
Huntington, WV 25701
(304) 523-3447

Contact Kanawha Valley
Christ Church United Methodist
Quarrier and Morris Streets
Charlestown, WV 25301
(304) 346-0828

Greenbriar Valley Mental
  Health Clinic
100 Church Street
Lewisburg, WV 24901
(304) 645-3319

Prestera Center for Mental
  Health Services
3375 U.S. Route 60 E.
PO Box 8069
Huntington, WV 25705
(304) 525-7851

Southern Highlands Community
  Mental Health Center
12th Street Extension
Princeton, WV 24740
(304) 425-9541

Upper Ohio Valley Crisis Hotline
PO Box 653
Wheeling, WV 26003
(304) 234-1848

WISCONSIN

Appleton Crisis Intervention
Center
3365 W. Brewster
Appleton, WI 54914
(414) 735-5354

Crisis Intervention Center/
Fond Du Lac
459 E. 1st Street
Fond Du Lac, WI 54935
(414) 929-3500

Crisis Intervention Center/
Manitowoc Area
131 S. Madison Street
Green Bay, WI 54301
(414) 432-7855

Crisis Intervention Center/
Oshkosh
PO Box 1411
Oshkosh, WI 54902
(414) 233-7709

Danes County Mental
Health Center
31 S. Henry
Madison, WI 53703
(608) 251-2341

Lakeland Community Center
P.O. Box 1005
Elkhorn, WI 53121
(414) 723-5400

Milwaukee County Crisis
Intervention Service
Mental Health Emergency Service
8770 W. Wisconsin Avenue K
Road
Milwaukee, WI 53226
(414) 271-2810

Suicide Prevention Center
1221 Whipple Street
Eau Claire, WI 54701
(715) 839-3274

WYOMING

Casper Suicide Prevention
611 Thelm Drive
Casper, WY 82609
(307) 234-5061

Cheyenne Helpline
PO Box 404
Cheyenne, WY 82001
(307) 632-4132

APPENDIX

APPENDIX A

ACRONYMS

AAS: American Association of Suicidology

AMA: American Medical Association

ASF: American Suicide Foundation

ECT: Electroconvulsive therapy

HHS: Health and Human Services

MAO: Monoamine oxidase

NCYSP: National Committee on Youth Suicide Prevention

NIMH: National Institute of Mental Health

TCA: Tricyclic antidepressant

WHO: World Health Organization

YSNC: Youth Suicide National Center

APPENDIX B

GLOSSARY

This glossary provides brief definitions of the basic terms encountered in the issues of suicide and euthanasia. Italics denote words or expressions covered in separate entries.

active euthanasia: The act of directly intervening to end a person's life, such as administering a lethal drug to a terminal patient. Active euthanasia is also referred to as *assisted suicide*.

assisted suicide: A suicide where the individual is aided in taking his own life by another person. The term "assisted suicide" is often used interchangeably with *active euthanasia*.

autocide: A suicide disguised as an automobile accident. Autocide is not the same as suicide with an automobile. The term refers to instances where individuals kill themselves in apparent automobile accidents to hide the fact of their suicide.

cluster suicides: The phenomenon where one person's suicide triggers other similar self-destructive acts in the same locale. The term is normally used to describe a series of youth suicides in the same area.

death with dignity: The concept that a person has a right to die without being subjected to intrusive and dehumanizing medical procedures.

euthanasia: From the ancient Greek *eu thanatos*, or "good death," the practice of ending life in an easy and painless way. Euthanasia is usually divided into two types: *active euthanasia* and *passive euthanasia*.

irreversible coma: A medical condition where a person is permanently unconscious and unaware.

living will: A document executed by an individual that expresses, in advance, medical treatment preferences in the event of an injury or illness that leaves the person unable to communicate. Normally a living will is used to indicate a desire not to be kept alive through artificial life-support measures.

mercy death: The same as *euthanasia.*

mercy killing: The unrequested taking of another person's life in order to spare the individual further suffering.

passive euthanasia: The act of allowing an individual to die from natural causes. The term is used to describe the withholding or withdrawal of life-support equipment from people who require such systems.

persistent vegetative state: A medical condition in which a person no longer has any meaningful brain activity. The person may appear to have sleep/wake cycles, but is completely unaware.

postvention: A term used to describe the various actions taken to assist persons who have been affected by a suicide or suicide attempt. This includes family members, friends, and associates as well as suicidal individuals themselves.

psychological autopsy: A technique used to help determine the cause of death. In instances where suicide is the suspected cause of death, experts examine the deceased's psychological history in order to make a final determination. The psychological autopsy is also an important research tool in discovering why a person committed suicide.

right to die: The idea that a person has a right to choose death in certain instances. The term is most often used to describe an individual's right to refuse artificial life-support measures.

serotonin: A kind of neurotransmitter, or chemical messenger, in the brain. Low levels of serotonin have been linked to depression and, less directly, to suicide.

suicide: The act of intentionally and deliberately taking one's own life.

suicide rate: The percentage of persons in a specific group who take their own lives in a given year. The rate is expressed per 100,000 population. A suicide rate of 15 means there were 15 suicides for every 100,000 people in this group.

suicidology: The study of suicide, including its nature, causes, prevention, and treatment.

terminal illness: An incurable medical condition that will lead to a patient's death within a relatively short time.

thanatology: The study of death and dying and the associated medical, psychological, and social issues.

INDEX

Index

Index

Index

Index

Index

Index